WPP

当代领袖 THE THOUGHTS OF CHAIRMEN NOW

Wisdom from China's business leaders and entrepreneurs

In a remarkable series of candid conversations, diverse leaders discuss the challenges as China rebalances following 30 years of high-octane growth. Added research and analysis, informed by our extensive China experience, yield unique insights for achieving sustained business success in this shifting landscape.

Printed in the UK by Butler Tanner and Dennis Ltd

ISBN 978-0-9571958-2-0
A catalogue record for this book is available from the British Library.

CONTENTS

PREFACE

OVERVIEW

THE CHAIRMEN
AND THEIR COMPANIES

CONTACTS & CREDITS

PREFACE

欢迎
Welcome

WELCOME TO "THE THOUGHTS OF CHAIRMEN NOW: WISDOM FROM CHINA'S BUSINESS LEADERS AND ENTREPRENEURS."

China is rebalancing.

After 30 years of unprecedented economic expansion, the new leadership seeks to realise a "Chinese Dream" that pairs more evenly paced growth with widely shared prosperity, domestic harmony and global stature.

What does this "national rejuvenation" mean for companies doing business in China?

Questions are more abundant than answers. But with over 30 years of combined experience living and working in China, we believe that in a time of transition it's most important to ask the right questions of the most knowledgeable people.

欢迎

Welcome

Jonathan Geldart
Jonathan.Geldart@gti.gt.com

David Roth
droth@wpp.com

Welcome to *The Thoughts of Chairmen Now: Wisdom from China's business leaders and entrepreneurs.*

With the benefit of unusual access, we addressed our questions to C-Suite executives from 14 important Chinese companies. Our book takes you into these candid meetings as business leaders share insights about the changing China, the strategies and tactics they employ and the prerequisites and subtleties required for sustained business success.

We believe that *The Thoughts of Chairmen Now* is essential reading for anyone planning to enter China or currently doing business there. It's also beneficial for Chinese executives, analysts, journalists, academics and anyone else interested in the unfiltered thinking of Chinese business leaders.

You'll learn not only what Chinese business leaders think, but also how they think and why deeply understanding business in China requires viewing it through the prism of Chinese history and culture. Topics covered include:

- Attitudes of management and the workforce and how they're shaped by China's history and culture.

- Opportunities and barriers facing Chinese brands as they expand at home and abroad.

- Challenges of rapid growth, such as the need for an educated workforce qualified to deal with complexity and change.

- Values guiding business leaders, including honesty, hard work and serving both individual and communal wellbeing.

- Leadership approaches for fostering staff devotion and more open communication.

Clarity and balance

We're grateful to each of the 14 leaders and to the many other experts and advisors, who contributed their time and knowledge to this important project. They share a desire to present China with clarity and balance and provide a realistic appraisal of how doing business in China compares with other markets.

They also share a need to improve the image of "Brand China." Many of these companies are present overseas or plan to be in the near future. International expansion success depends in part on "Brand China," the image of the country and the reputation of Chinese goods and services.

For these leaders, this book is a platform to address preconceptions well expressed by He Fulong, chairman of ITG, a major conglomerate. "People misunderstand China," he told us. "Some people take a political position and demonise China. Others take a more cultural view and mythologise China. Both of these perspectives are limited and distorted."

How to achieve a comprehensive and undistorted perspective? For us, the hours we spent with each of the Chinese leaders were illuminating and an exciting first step. These conversations form the heart of the book, which we divided into 14 sections, one for each company. Each section features a summary of the company, a profile of the leader and an interview Q&A.

And because the deepest understanding of Chinese companies comes from being in China, from personally interacting and seeing the country with your own eyes, we illustrated the book with remarkable photos to capture the essence of the businesses and the personalities that lead them.

We also added relevant commentary, including exclusive market research and analysis from Millward Brown China, a WPP company and BrandZ™, WPP's brand equity and analytics database.

Finally, to make the extensive material maximally useful and accessible, we organised it into relevant themes that appear in a series of analytical Overview essays and prescriptive Take Aways. We also included contact details at the back of the book for additional help and information.

Next steps

Appreciating China in all its diversity and complexity is critical for business success. We intended *The Thoughts of Chairmen Now* to reflect this appreciation and inspire further inquiry. For the specific strategic insights that can help assure your business success in China we invite you to turn to us—and the extensive experience we represent.

To learn more about building a business in China, contact Grant Thornton Zhi Tong. With our "one China, one firm" approach, we work together seamlessly across China and Hong Kong, forming a network of 17 offices with access to 120 partners and over 2,700 professionals. We serve a broad base of clients including over 150 public companies and more than 2,000 SOEs (Stated Owned Enterprises), private companies and MNCs (Multinational Companies).

To learn more about building brands in China, contact WPP. Located in Shanghai, Beijing, Guangzhou and many other cities and provinces, WPP companies—with all our significant resources, including over 14,000 employees in Greater China—are here to help you gain competitive advantage. We offer insights, advertising, digital, PR, promotion, marketing, media, retail and shopper marketing—the knowledge and implementation necessary to understand China and build and sustain brand value.

We believe that you'll enjoy *The Thoughts of Chairmen Now* and find it immensely useful to consider the collective wisdom of China's business leaders and entrepreneurs. The remaining challenge is using this wisdom to full advantage. For the name and contact details of someone who can assist you, please reach out to the China experts listed at the end of the book, or feel free to contact either of us directly.

OVERVIEW

INTRODUCTION

OPTIMISTIC AND DETERMINED, CHAIRMEN FACE NEW CHALLENGES

The business leaders we interviewed for this book do not speak with one voice.

The 14 men and women are a diverse group, varying in age, temperament, background, industry, leadership style, geographic region and the kind of company they manage, which range from large and state owned to small and entrepreneurial.

Some began their careers before the period of opening and reform initiated by Deng Xiaoping in the late 1970s. Others were children at that time and spent their early adult years studying abroad. They spoke to us at a decisive moment, as the government evaluated progress halfway through China's twelfth Five-Year Plan.

The leaders provided a business perspective. Their experiences and viewpoints yielded insights about the complicated Chinese business universe today, during a transition period marked by new national leadership, a slowdown in the rate of economic growth and the pivot from an economy driven by manufacturing to one driven by services and domestic consumption.

How these business leaders and entrepreneurs address the growing affluence and sophistication of Chinese consumers in both the major and lower tier cities, build their company brands and burnish and redefine the reputation of "Brand China" will have global repercussions and especially impact companies doing business with China.

They share in common an optimistic determination to navigate this period of economic and social rebalancing and succeed not simply for personal gain but also for the benefit of their companies, their employees and the future of China.

Preparing for future growth

"The country's image will impact the level of investment we receive," said Gong Yuegiong, vice president at Foton, the car and truck maker. "China will need to change over the next 10 years so that we are accepted globally and can market our products."

These changes include the need to restore eroded consumer trust; strengthen the critical thinking skills of the workforce; and balance growth with respect for heritage. The erosion of trust follows 30 years of rapid growth whose unintended consequences include traffic congestion, air and water pollution and food safety hazards, problems facing many industrial economies.

The executives don't blame the government for these problems. But they expect the government to work collaboratively with business to find solutions. Alice Fan Yang, of NCAM, which manages insurance company assets, reflected philosophically on a well-known Chinese saying: "There are no fish in clear water," meaning impurities are a natural by-product of life.

"Companies need to take a breather," said David Sun, chief executive of Home Inns, the hotel chain. "They need time to make improvements and refinements to help ensure that the next fast-growth period will be healthier." Reflecting on the current period of rebalancing, he added, "This is a national problem."

Educating the workforce

When Sun outlined plans to double in size to 5,000 hotels over the next eight-to-10 years, he emphasised the need to find people who are capable of making decisions in a large, multi-brand enterprise.

The problem for Alice Fan Yang is finding qualified people who understand complicated insurance products, because prospective employees too often are poorly educated, having migrated recently from countryside to city. "It requires selecting people who have reached a certain level of schooling and then educating them about insurance," she said.

To an extent, the labour shortage in a land of over 1.3 billion inhabitants is a symptom of success. As affluence spreads there's less incentive for people to seek employment in cities, where wages are rising, but at a slower pace than the cost of living. The government's urbanisation policy may help correct the imbalance. As industries move to lower tier cities, China's wealth, infrastructure, education, medical care and other benefits will become more equitably distributed.

Over half of China's population now lives in cities compared with less than 20 per cent in 1980. Rapid urbanisation altered the character of many Chinese cities. Reminders of the country's long history disappeared as progress took priority over preservation. "Slow is not necessarily better," said Chairman He Fulong of ITG, a conglomerate, "but moving too fast can be like pulling on a plant to help it grow."

Strengthening "Brand China"

All of these issues impact "Brand China," which encapsulates China's core values, the quality of its products and its reliability as a partner. For Chinese business leaders, impressions of China will determine how easily their companies can find receptive markets, access to capital and strategic acquisition investments.

They expect "Brand China" to propel growth not inhibit it. "The government will need to continue addressing challenges, such as narrowing the gap between rich and poor people," said Gong, vice president of Foton, the motor vehicle manufacturer.

The goal is not to imitate the West, however. Regardless of their age or background, the executives see China as different in important ways from developed economies, particularly those in the northern half of the western hemisphere. China's people are more industrious and willing to place the common welfare above personal wellbeing, they say.

Similarly, in our conversation with the Chinese business leaders, we were struck by how their priorities differed from those we often hear from executives. They spoke less about sales and profits and more about being exemplary organisations that achieve commercial success with modesty, frugality and respect for all constituents—employees, the local community, shareholders, customers and the state.

Employees reciprocate with loyalty to company that imitates devotion to family. From our perspective, this phenomenon potentially provides a competitive advantage over businesses from the West, where the primacy of the individual and greater affluence reduces mutual commitment.

China and the West

We observed key differences in Chinese and western business operating styles, too. In Chinese companies, the effort to achieve consensus can slow the launch of new initiatives. But once out of the gate, Chinese companies can execute nimbly, pragmatically and at lightning speed. They excel at adapting and managing risk on the run.

The executives suggested that Chinese businesses could learn more about formal planning from the West. We believe that a fusion of western planning cycles with Chinese executional adeptness would produce

management best practices that are neither eastern nor western, but rather universal.

Confucianism, Buddhism and other influences during 5,000 years of history have shaped Chinese ways. Imperialism and the hardships endured during the past two centuries inform the relationship with the West. The desire to engage is also influenced by the belief that China's cultural distinctiveness needs to be reclaimed and protected.

From our interviews and analysis it's clear that the country is changing and those seeking to do business with China will engage both with business leaders whose careers began 30 years ago, at the dawn of China's economic reform and those of the next generation. All are adjusting to the current period of social and economic rebalancing.

We also found general agreement on this point: People in the West understand little about China and its long and complicated past. Complete knowledge of this history is neither possible nor expected. Some knowledge, however, is a necessary context for doing business in China. Pursuing it with humility is a gateway to deep personal relationships on which sustained business success depends.

"China is neither as terrible and chaotic as some people allege, nor is it as great as other people assert," said ITG Chairman He. "The reality is in the middle. China is moving forward continuously."

Jonathan and David

Jonathan Geldart
Global Head - Marketing Communications,
Grant Thornton International Ltd.
Jonathan.Geldart@gti.gt.com

David Roth
CEO, The Store WPP
Europe, Middle East, Africa (EMEA) and Asia
droth@wpp.com

INTRODUCTION

China's Journey Through History

PART 1: 5,000 YEARS

The contributions of Chinese civilisation over 5,000 years advanced culture, science and medicine, philosophy, technology, commerce and the art of governance, enriching the entire world. This engagement brought China both peace and conflict.

Following the Shang, the Zhou Dynasty expands its territorial control, establishes a permanent capital and appoints local administrators to help govern.

> **FROM THE FIRST EMPEROR TO THE HAN**
> **CONFUCIUS, DAOISM AND THE SILK ROAD**
> **600 - CE**

As the local administrators gain strength, they compete for power in the Warring States Period. New philosophies emerge during this disruption. Confucius is born in 551 and Laozi, the founder of Daoism, is born at around the same time.

The Xia people lead China during part of the Bronze Age, followed by the Shang and the Zhou. The Shang build cities and advance the Chinese written language with elaborate inscriptions on turtle shells and animal bones.

When the Qin people emerge as the strongest state, King Ying Zheng proclaims himself the First Emperor and establishes the Qin Dynasty, in 221. He promotes unity with centralised administration, simplified language, a common currency and roads. Existing fortifications are connected to become the Great Wall. The famous terracotta warriors guard the tomb of the First Emperor.

Following a civil war, the Han Dynasty ascends in 206 and rules for around 400 years. The Han establish a civil service meritocracy for governing the country. As the Han expand westward, overland routes known as the Silk Road facilitate trade. Chinese silk and other products reach Europe.

Agricultural society emerges.

2000 to 1050

206 Han Dynasty

221 The First Emperor

BEFORE THE
COMMON ERA
(BCE)

551 Confucius

1050 to 600

BUDDHISM ARRIVES IN CHINA
THE TANG FOSTER PEACE AND PROSPERITY
CE - 1000

Monks travelling the Silk Road introduce Buddhism to China during the early years of the Common Era.

As the Han Dynasty weakens, the empire splits apart and China enters a period of strife that lasts almost 400 years.

China is reunified in 581, under the Sui Dynasty. Although in power for less than 40 years, the Sui link waterways to create the Grand Canal for transporting grain.

Starting in 618, The Tang Dynasty presides over a long peaceful period of great prosperity, medical and scientific advancement, international trade and artistic development.

Chang'an, the imperial capital located at the eastern end of the Silk Road, becomes a cosmopolitan city of around one million inhabitants.

Internal rivalries lead to the decline of the Tang Dynasty and 50 years of disunity that ends in 960, with the ascension of the Song Dynasty.

THE MONGOLS AND THE MING
TRADE AND INDUSTRY EXPAND
1000 - 1500

The Song Dynasty rules China for over 300 hundred years, strengthens the central government and improves the quality of administration by using exams to select the best bureaucrats. Paper money is introduced during the Song period.

Landscape painting and calligraphy emerge as important art forms. Influential scientific developments include the invention of gunpowder, moveable type for printing and the compass for navigation.

Genghis Khan unites the peoples of the northern grasslands and establishes the Mongol Empire in 1206. Military conquests connect the Pacific with the Mediterranean.

Kublai Khan, grandson of Genghis Khan, conquers the Song and establishes the Yuan Dynasty, in 1271. The Yuan divide China into administrative units, the model for today's provinces and prefectures. Marco Polo visits China during this period.

With the demise of the Mongols, the Ming Dynasty is established during the fourteenth century. The Ming set their capital at the site known today as Beijing and complete construction of the Forbidden City, in 1421. They implement a national postal system and renovate the Great Wall and the Grand Canal.

In long voyages of exploration the Ming sail to India and as far as Arabia and Africa.

584 The Grand Canal

100 Buddhism

1368 Ming Dynasty

1206 Mongol Empire

960 Song Dynasty

COMMON ERA (CE)

618 Tang Dynasty

THE MANCHUS FORM THE QING DYNASTY
TRADE BRINGS WEALTH AND CONFLICT
1500 - 1911

Jesuit missionaries and Dutch, Portuguese and Spanish merchants expand western influence. International trade grows along the coast, enriching China with silver.

Ultimately, a silver shortage is among the internal pressures that, along with the external threat of Manchu power in the northeast, weaken Ming authority. China's population reaches around 200 million by the end of the Ming Dynasty in 1644.

The Manchus form the Qing Dynasty in 1644 and over several decades gain control of China, which the Qing Dynasty rules until 1911.

Western demand for Chinese tea, silk, porcelain and other goods increases. With the industrial revolution, Great Britain and other nations seek new overseas markets. Initially, the Qing limit trade with the West to the port at Canton. Opium grown in India becomes Britain's largest export to China.

Two wars erupt during the nineteenth century as China attempts to curtail the opium trade. The 1842 Treaty of Nanjing ends the first Opium War and forces China to open more ports along its east coast.

The Taiping religious sect gains followers in southern and central China. Advocating for social reform, the Taiping attempt to overthrow the Qing Dynasty. Millions of people die before the Qing Dynasty ends the civil war in 1864.

A group called the Yi He Tuan organises against the presence of foreigners and foreign powers. Also called Boxers because many followers practice martial arts, the group attacks foreign diplomatic offices in Beijing. Neutral at first, the government eventually supports the Boxers.

After foreign troops quash the Boxer Rebellion, a 1901 peace treaty forces China to pay long-term reparations to Russia, Germany, France, Great Britain, Japan, Italy, Austria–Hungary and the United States.

1850 Civil War

1842 Treaty of Nanjing

1901 Boxer Rebellion

1644 Qing Dynasty

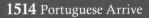

1514 Portuguese Arrive

1911

China's Journey Through History

PART 2: THE LAST CENTURY

In the century since dynastic rule ended in 1911, China reintroduced itself to the world. Today, faced with the challenges of modern life, it summons ancient wisdom to construct a society that is prosperous, equitable and Chinese.

THE END OF DYNASTIC RULE BIRTH OF THE PEOPLE'S REPUBLIC 1911 - 1949

The demise of the Qing, in 1911, ends four millennia of dynastic rule in China. A provisional government is established the following year. Sun Yatsen's National People's Party, also known as the Guomingdang, gains majority representation and names Sun president.

Sun Yatsen's rivals attempt to restore imperial China and soon exile Sun. China drifts without firm central leadership until Sun returns.

Sun Yatsen reorganises the Guomingdang based on the Bolshevik model. Mao Zedong and others form the Chinese Communist Party in 1921. The two groups initially work together.

Following the death of Sun Yatsen, in 1925, Chiang Kaishek assumes leadership of the Guomindang. A long struggle for control ensues between the Guomingdang and the Red Army of the Communist Party.

In the mid-1930s, Mao evades the much larger Guomindang forces by leading an estimated 115,000 Communist troops on a 6,000-mile journey to northern China. Few survive the Long March.

Japanese forces brutally attack Nanjing and its citizens.

Japanese invasion and World War II interrupt the power struggle between the Nationalists and the Communists. When the struggle resumes after the war the Communists gain strength and the Nationalists retreat to Taiwan.

Mao establishes the People's Republic of China on October 1, 1949 and leads China for a quarter-century.

FROM THE GREAT LEAP FORWARD TO INTERNATIONAL DIPLOMACY 1950 - 1979

The Great Leap Forward, during the late 1950s, attempts to accelerate economic development, but leads to severe food shortages.

Mao inaugurates the Cultural Revolution in 1966.

In 1971, the UN recognises the People's Republic as one of the five permanent members of the Security Council.

China and the United States move to normalise relations following the meeting of Chairman Mao and President Nixon in 1972.

Deng Xiaoping emerges as China's leader after Mao's death in 1976.

Deng launches a policy of reform and opening up to restore China's economic vitality and engage with other nations.

1931 The Long March

1921 Communist Party

1911 Empire Ends

20TH CENTURY

1978 Opening Up

1971 Security Council

1958 Great Leap Forward

1949 PRC Founded

1937 Nanjing Assault

ECONOMIC REFORM AND GROWTH
RAPID RISE IN PROSPERITY
1980 - 1999

Deng encourages foreign investment with practical steps like creating the first four Special Economic Zones on China's southeast coast.

The economy expands steadily through the 1980s, with the annual GDP (Gross Domestic Product) growth rate averaging around 9 per cent.

The historic Shanghai Stock Exchange is reopened and the Shenzhen Stock Exchange is established.

In 1992, with the economy lagging, Deng promotes his policies on what becomes known as the Southern Tour. The economy responds and annual growth of GDP spikes to over 14 per cent. Deng dies in 1997.

Britain returns Hong Kong to China in 1997, more than 150 years after taking control following the First Opium War. Macau is transferred from Portuguese sovereignty to China in 1999.

THE NEXT MILLENNIUM
A NEW "CHINESE DREAM"
2000 TO PRESENT

China joins the World Trade Organisation in 2001, signalling the country's international economic importance and engagement.

Astronaut Yang Liwei orbits the earth in the Shenzhou 5 spacecraft, making China only the third country engaged in manned space flight.

GDP climbs steadily, peaking at 14.2 per cent growth in 2007, just before the global financial crisis.

China hosts the 2008 Summer Olympics. The opening ceremonies and the games showcase China's achievements.

In 2009, China overtakes the United States as the world's largest car market.

With a GDP of $5.9 trillion, according to the World Bank, China surpasses Japan to become the world's second largest economy after the United States.

China leads the world in Internet users (591 million) and number of mobile phones (1.2 billion), in 2013.

Xi Jinping succeeds Hu Jintao as China's president, in 2013, with a promise to advance the "Chinese Dream" of sustained prosperity for a growing middle class.

1997 Hong Kong

1992 Southern Tour

1990 Stock Exchanges

1980 Economic Zones

2010 Economic Power

2008 Beijing Olympics

2003 Space Orbit

2001 WTO

2013 "Chinese Dream"

21ST CENTURY

THOUGHTS ON BRAND

CHINESE BRANDS AND "BRAND CHINA," DRIVE GROWTH AT HOME AND ABROAD

Chinese companies are increasingly engaged in brand building.

Brand is now on the CEO agenda in a way that it was not just five years ago, our discussions with Chinese business leaders revealed. They recognise that in a changing economy, price is not an enduring discriminator and that a brand's intangible value has many tangible benefits.

As Chinese consumers become more discerning, meaningful brand differentiation enables them to assess brand benefits and navigate choice. Brand also becomes an important instrument to inspire employees and build awareness.

The focus on brand applies not only to entrepreneurial businesses, but even to the SOEs (State Owned Enterprises). While primarily focussed on extending their brands throughout China's enormous domestic market, more companies also understand the importance of brand for fulfilling international ambitions.

"We used to think of brand as only communication," said Gong Yueqiong, vice president of Foton, the maker of cars and trucks. "But we understand brand differently now. It's embedded in our strategy and execution, into everything that we do."

Gong expects to build Foton into a global brand over time, with initial attention on developing markets like India and Brazil, which are well suited for the brand's proposition of quality at an affordable price. But China is the priority for now.

Building domestic presence also is the focus for Home Inns, the fastest-growing Chinese

hotel brand, with around 2,000 hotels. But the company's plans to operate 5,000 hotels worldwide in the next eight-to-10 years depend on leveraging the power of its brand.

"Currently, about 80 million Chinese people travel overseas annually," said Home Inns chief executive, David Sun. "That number should almost double in the next 10 years. We need to build loyalty to the brand. That's critical for expansion globally. You need to go overseas with your customers. They carry the brand with them."

Improving "Brand China"

Part of the challenge in building a Chinese brand abroad is the international reputation of "Brand China." Perceptions of particular national aptitudes—German engineering or Italian design, for example— can enhance brands. In contrast, China's image can compound the brand building challenge.

"The world disapproves of China," said Gong Weibin, CEO of Refond, the LED lighting manufacturer. "The West sees China as a communist country, so it's biased towards things that come from China."

The personality of "Brand China" is characterised as innocent, friendly, kind and caring, based on analysis powered by WPP's BrandZ™ brand analytic database. As the Chinese brands seek greater acceptance, both at home and abroad, the nation will need to strengthen the "Brand China" personality.

To help power the global presence of Chinese brands, "Brand China" will need to sharpen other characteristics, such as being perceived as trustworthy and wise and offering quality. To compete in the luxury car sector the brands will need to strengthen their emotional appeal and badge status.

"China will need to change over the next 10 years so that we are accepted globally and can market our products," said Gong, the Foton executive. "Our partners will need to feel that doing business with China is no more difficult than doing business in the West."

What's in a name

Characteristically, Chinese brands often are layered with meaning contained in the Chinese characters that express the name. Yanjing was the name of one of China's ancient capital cities located on the spot today occupied by Beijing, the beer's strongest market.

The brand's global ambitions are embedded in a two-part slogan: "Inspire the world. Exceed the dream." Each part of the slogan is intended to convey several meanings, according to Chairman Li Fucheng.

The word inspire, for example refers to the rapid growth of China during the past 30 years, the country's rise in international athletic competition and the rapid growth of the Yanjing brand. Yanjing sponsored a week long event in London during the 2012 Summer Olympics and was an official sponsor of the 2008 Beijing Olympics.

Safewell, the manufacturer of safes and security devices, relied on feng shui to create a name, which in Chinese is Shengwei.

"Sheng" means strong and "wei" means prestige. "Sheng" is similar to the sound "shen" in Chinese, which means kidneys, considered a foundation of good health.

The name of the motor vehicle company Futon comes from the Chinese words fu and tian. The character fu means good fortune and is ubiquitous during the Chinese New Year. When combined with the character tian, which means fields, the name implies much good fortune.

Huayi, the large chemical and pharmaceutical SOE, is unifying many sub-brands under the Huayi name, even eliminating well-established brands to strengthen the impact of the Huayi master brand. "The Group does not compete with enterprises for profit and the enterprises do not compete with the Group for name," said Chairman Liu Xunfeng.

Huayi maintains substantial international brand presence through 34 joint ventures with global chemical and pharmaceutical companies. Said Liu, "I think that all Chinese businesses in the future will emphasise brand if they want to achieve sustained success."

Chinese and Multinational Brand Character Perceptions

To build their brands outside of China and compete effectively with western brands, across categories, Chinese brands need to strengthen the brand character perception that they are trustworthy and wise.

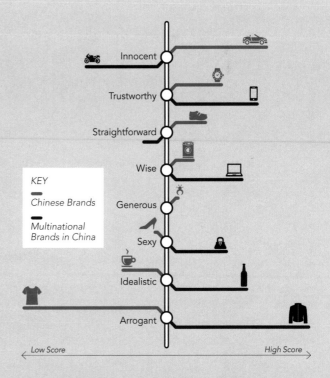

KEY

— Chinese Brands

▬ Multinational Brands in China

Innocent
Trustworthy
Straightforward
Wise
Generous
Sexy
Idealistic
Arrogant

Low Score → High Score

Source: Millward Brown, a WPP company

THOUGHTS ON COMMUNICATION

沟通
Communication

LEADERS BALANCE SUBTLETY AND THE MIDDLE WAY WITH NEED FOR MORE CLARITY AND OPENNESS

Alice Fan Yang had to relearn how to cross the streets of Beijing.

Born and raised in China, she studied and worked in the West. During her years abroad, Yang became accustomed to relatively well-regulated western life, symbolised for her by traffic lights that drivers reliably obey.

Beijing traffic seemed chaotic to Yang when she returned home. It took time for her to acclimatise, sense the rhythm and unexpressed rules of the road and feel comfortable stepping into traffic and navigating through it.

"In China, even if the light is green, it's not necessarily your signal to safely cross. You need to make some judgments," said Yang, assistant president of NCAM, an asset management company. "And those judgments are based on experience. If you expect western rules, you may not like what you see."

Encouraging more directness

If simple activities like crossing the street can be hard to comprehend, conducting intricate business transactions can be fraught with cues missed or misconstrued.

Smart Chinese business executives are trying to minimise this problem by creating conditions where employees feel more comfortable speaking openly. These recent initiatives reflect one of the most significant shifts in attitude that we discerned in our conversations with business leaders.

When Chairman He Fulong of ITG, a conglomerate, asked 18 senior managers to assess the near-term prospects for the Chinese economy by answering simply, better, worse, or unsure, for example, no one said that the business would be worse.

"I realised that some who responded positively to my poll may have held a different opinion," said He. "This response in part reflects their Chinese manner." According to David Sun, chief executive of Home Inns, "One of the hardest challenges is what Westerners say, 'You never know what the Chinese people are thinking.'"

NUANCE INSIGHT

[Enterprise / Business]

企 is a composite character, as many Chinese characters are. On top is the character 人, which means people; below is the character 止, which means stop. The literal interpretation seems to be that without the people that comprise an enterprise everything will grind to a halt. The inference is that people are fundamental to the welfare of any organisation.

"Sometimes Chinese people don't know what their colleagues are thinking," said Sun. "So the biggest challenge is to create an environment where people feel that they can be open."

Chinese written and spoken communication evolved over 5,000 years of civilisation, from traditions that strive for a middle way, a balance and harmony among participants, rather than the winners and losers that can emerge from the western adversarial approach.

Communication reflects thinking

"The Chinese way of doing business is built on Confucian and Buddhist thinking," said Chairman Wang Longchu, of the Xiangyu Group, a conglomerate, "We think from the inside to the outside, the middle way."

Ideal employees act according to Buddhist and Confucian teachings. While they're self-confident and take risks, according to Li Fucheng, chairman of Yanjing Beer, "At the same time, they carry out their duties with modesty and frugality. These employees are able to win the customer's heart and sustain our strong brand."

A company might reinforce this behaviour, but it's rooted deeply in the Chinese psyche and implicit in the language itself. Chinese characters are not simply symbols for sounds, like a western alphabet. Rather, they're embedded with ideas.

In noting the centrality of people in Chinese companies, for example, He Fulong, of ITG, explained that the Chinese character for business is comprised of the symbol for people over the symbol for stop, implying that a company ultimately is about people and nothing happens without them.

"China and the West differ in many areas, which is very normal and understandable," said Hu Shoushan, the CEO of Fuxing Huiyu, a real estate development company. "However, I hope western people will look at eastern culture in a rational and reasonable way."

CHINA

AT A GLANCE

Key Facts and Figures

Geography

Land Area

9.6 million km²/3.7 million mi²

China is one of the world's largest countries in land area, smaller than Russia and roughly equivalent in size to Canada and the United States.

Urbanisation

More than half of China's population lives in cities today compared with less than 20 per cent when the period of opening up and economic reform began in 1980.

| 19% | 26% | 36% |
| 1980 | 1990 | 2000 |

| 49% | 52% |
| 2010 | 2012 |

Per cent of the population living in urban settings

People

Population

1.35 billion (2013)

Median Age

36.3 years

The number of people over age 60 will double during the next 20 years and China will face the challenges of an ageing society. The recent relaxation of the one child policy by government may help in the long term but the challenge of an ageing population will be present for at least a generation, possibly two in China.

Employment

Employment to population ratio 71%

Of China's population of people age 15 or over, 71 per cent are employed, compared with 58 per cent in the United States; the United Kingdom, 57 per cent; India, 54 per cent or Brazil, 65 per cent (2011).

Women in the workforce 51%

China leads the world in the number of senior management positions held by women, 51 per cent, compared with a global average of 24 per cent.

Sources: Grant Thornton International Business Report, The World Bank, National Bureau of Statistics of China, China Internet Network Information Center, The World Fact Book (CIA), CNRS-TGI

THOUGHTS ON CORPORATE RESPONSIBILITY

责任
Responsibility

INDIVIDUAL AND CORPORATE WEALTH ARE GOOD, BUT MUST SERVE SOCIETY

Judging from the unprecedented rise of several hundred million people into the middle class and an unquenchable desire for western luxury brands, it might seem as if accumulating personal wealth has been China's sole motivation during the past 30 years of rapid economic growth.

It might seem that way, but as is often the case in China, the surface appearance may be wrong, misleading or only a thin slice of a much more nuanced and complicated story.

The Chinese have a long association with money. They introduced paper currency to the world during the Song Dynasty, in around 1000 CE (Common Era). Chinese merchants traded internationally, along the Silk Road, starting roughly 200 BCE (Before the Common Era), during the Han Dynasty. For much of China's population, the only novelty about money during the past three decades was having some.

As in the West, China's market economy tries to balance—and now rebalance— the needs of the individual with those of the wider society. The Chinese, however, mediate the ideas of Adam Smith with the teachings of the Buddha, Confucius and other Chinese thinkers. Consumption is only one aspect of a "Chinese Dream" for a more stable, prosperous and equitable society.

"The leaders of businesses in China have a lot of heart for what they do," said Wang Xianrong, chairwoman of C&D, a holding company. "The Chinese people will put their energy and efforts into what they do. It's not just for the money. They want to realise their dreams and do something valuable for China."

Improving society

Wang Zhenghua left a career in government service to open a travel agency during the 1980s, the earliest years of Deng Xiaoping's economic reforms. Today, Wang operates one of China's most successful travel agencies and Spring Airlines, a low-cost carrier. At age 70, making money remains important, but making air travel affordable to more people is the goal that really excites him.

"China has many low-income people who have never flown on an airplane," said Wang. "It is my dream to help them fly."

Around a decade after Wang Zhenghua left government, Wang Kaixue left his job as a professor of engineering. He's now president of CITMS, a transportation technology company. The career shift happened unexpectedly when Wang encountered an opportunity to create surveillance systems that monitor vehicle traffic and reduce congestion, improving the quality of city life.

He views himself as part of the "Generation of '92," a group of fellow entrepreneurs who started businesses around the time of Deng's famous "Southern Tour" to promote the success of the Special Economic Zones. Many members of the "Generation of '92" who became wealthy now find less satisfaction from making money than from contributing to the betterment of society.

"Originally, my colleagues and I thought about our company from a financial and business perspective," said Wang. "Later developments changed our thinking. And we realised that what we do is closely related to people's lives and wellbeing."

Paying taxes with a smile

In the West, successful entrepreneurs traditionally give back to society through foundations or some other mechanism that improves a favourite institution and often includes a naming opportunity. The funding supports the common good, while also promoting the individual.

Because of personal modesty and a system in which the state, not the private sector, is charged with taking care of the public welfare, Chinese entrepreneurs are less likely to use private wealth to build and name a hospital wing. "In China, if businesses really take their social responsibility seriously, then the government will distribute more resources and opportunities to them," said Wang of CITMS.

The commitment by businesses to the larger community is both an affirmation of Corporate Social Responsibility (CSR) and an extension of the centrality of family in Chinese society. The attitude toward paying taxes illustrates the contrast in western and Chinese approaches to building businesses and serving the greater good.

Expected to maximise return to stockholders, increase profit, elevate share prices and retain earnings for investment, western companies generally attempt to minimise their tax liability. That's not the practice in China.

"In measuring achievements, the hard KPIs (Key Performance Indicators) and financial data are just one side," said Li Fucheng, chairman of Yanjing Beer. "Another side is corporate responsibility." Included in Li's examples of corporate responsibility, along with caring for the environment and offering employment opportunities, is honouring the tax obligation.

"We are a big tax payer," he said with pride.

DEFINITIONS

State Owned Enterprises (SOEs)

Many of the companies studied in this report are State Owned Enterprises (SOEs), businesses run by the government.

China's central government runs almost 120 SOEs, according to the country's National Bureau of Statistics. At the same time, local governments operate numerous businesses, also considered as technically state owned.

SOEs often lead their product category in China and many enjoy global presence. With over 740 million subscribers, China Mobile is the world's largest telecom provider. It's China's most valuable brand, with a value of $50.6 billion, according to the BrandZ™ Top 50 Most Valuable Chinese Brands 2013. (www.brandz.com/china)

SOEs fall into these three classifications based on the extent of government ownership and control:

- **Pure SOE**: The state often owns these companies outright. Sometimes the state engages in joint ventures, but retains ultimate control.

  Examples: Petro China, Sinopec

- **State Holding Enterprise**: This category, where the state is a shareholder in a publicly traded company, divides into two parts: (a) Companies in which the state owns the majority of shares; and (b) Companies in which the state, as a minority shareholder, maintains control.

  Examples: (a) Wu Liang Ye (Baijiu liquor), (b) Yunnan Baiyao (healthcare)

- **State Owned Shareholding Enterprise**: In these publicly held companies, the state is neither a majority shareholder nor in control.

  Example: Ping An (financial services)

Based on how SOEs go to market, the BrandZ™ definition further divides companies into two types: Strategic and Competitive.

- **Strategic SOE**: These companies operate in categories, such as banking and oil and gas, which are important to China's national interests and are comprised mostly of other SOEs.

- **Competitive SOE**: These companies operate in categories, such as healthcare, food or liquor, where they face private entrepreneurial competitors. Market forces compel these SOEs to cultivate consumer loyalty and build brands.

Among China's largest businesses in sales turnover and brand value, SOEs comprised 74 per cent of value of the BrandZ™ Top 50 Most Valuable Chinese Brands 2013, down slightly from a year earlier. And as China's economy evolves, brand is becoming more important to consumers facing expanding choice in competitive industries and categories. Consequently, brand value is growing at a faster pace for Competitive SOEs and market-driven firms, compared with Strategic SOEs.

Brand Value Grows for Competitive SOEs

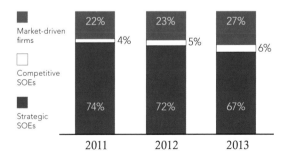

Reflecting the growing influence of Chinese consumers, brand value is increasing more rapidly for market-driven firms and competitive SOEs compared with strategic SOEs.

Source: BrandZ™ / Millward Brown, a WPP company

DEFINITIONS

City Tiers

For over 2,000 years, since the Qin Dynasty, China's rulers have attempted to organise the vast territory into a hierarchy of political entities.

The government today divides the People's Republic of China into five administrative divisions roughly based on geography and population: province, prefecture, county, township and village.

Separately and with some overlap, an unofficial system organises cities into tiers, based in part on size but mostly on economic development. The tier system is not definitive. Low tier cities include high-income people, for example and cities shift tiers as they change in size.

This fluidity, along with China's size and diversity, make it impossible to create a perfect system for categorising the nation's cities. Despite its shortcomings, the tier system is a useful classification device for companies attempting to understand and do business in a country as sprawling as China.

Research by Millward Brown, a WPP research company with a major presence in China, compares the city tiers by levels of Internet penetration, for example. The research highlights the disparities within China and the opportunities.

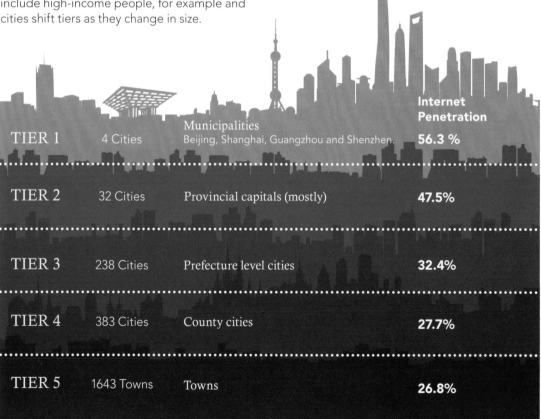

			Internet Penetration
TIER 1	4 Cities	Municipalities Beijing, Shanghai, Guangzhou and Shenzhen.	56.3 %
TIER 2	32 Cities	Provincial capitals (mostly)	47.5%
TIER 3	238 Cities	Prefecture level cities	32.4%
TIER 4	383 Cities	County cities	27.7%
TIER 5	1643 Towns	Towns	26.8%

Research and analysis by Millward Brown, a WPP company

TAKE AWAYS

见解
Explanation

INSIGHTS FOR SUSTAINED SUCCESS IN A REBALANCING CHINA

TAKE AWAYS

Culture

Culture

Seek the middle way

In the West the process for establishing business relationships often is adversarial, sometimes antagonistic, based on the assumption that best and most honest outcomes result when parties with competing interests directly and clearly advocate for their points of view. In China the process is about pursuing balance, finding a middle way. In the end, both western and Chinese business leaders seek a win-win resolution. Westerners will tend to focus on the engagement from their side of the chessboard. The Chinese executive may take more of a helicopter view, seeking arrangements that benefit everyone and leave all parties feeling respected.

Work for the communal welfare

In both the West and China people work to put food on the table. Both Westerners and Chinese people feel a complementary need to contribute to society in a way that results in personal fulfilment. Westerners often fill that need through volunteer work with civil or religious organisations. In China, where those kinds of organisations are less prevalent, the welfare of the larger community, what Western companies might term CSR (Corporate Social Responsibility), is fundamental to the corporate mission.

Expect complexity

Westerners expect clarity and are comfortable with unambiguous rules, a Ten Commandments "do this, don't do that" mentality. Chinese thinking evolved from philosophies and religions that provide directional guidelines for living but allow for more contradiction and ambiguity. The Chinese are comfortable in the grey area between black and white. Learning to navigate in these circumstances takes willingness to be patient, observant and non-judgmental. Deep understanding may not be possible, nor is it absolutely necessary because Chinese business people increasingly take the time to learn western ways. However, taking the time to understand Chinese ways can be rewarding, both professionally and personally.

Listen closely

Chinese communication can be layered and complicated. Words themselves may not only describe an object but also an attitude toward the object. The Chinese character for the word business, for example, is comprised of a symbol meaning people and another meaning stop, implying that the people are critical to an enterprise and nothing happens without them. In this instance and many others, the Chinese language expresses in one character what might require a sentence in a western language. Spoken Chinese can include the same kind of pregnant illusions present in written text. Comprehending Chinese is like appreciating a detailed Renaissance painting. It's laden with symbolic details that require time to recognise and decode. Anyone impatient to get to the point, may miss the point.

管理
Management

Management

Manage on the run

Western companies may be more comfortable dividing operations into two parts: planning and doing. Chinese tend to do both functions together and often do them well. They've perfected the art of managing on the run. Western companies generally are at a more mature stage of development. They're well organised, with corporate structure and process overseen by a chief executive who's usually a professional manager. Chinese companies sometimes lack comparable rules and regulations. While Chinese business leaders take a long-term view, they may run their organisations with less obvious strategic vision, but faster reaction time to meet the demands of the rapidly changing domestic market.

Reward industriousness

People work hard. They are motivated by new opportunities to rise into the middle class and enjoy basic products and even luxuries that were inaccessible to all but a few only a generation ago. Motivated by hard times in the recent past, the prospect of a better life and communal expectations, Chinese workers willingly put in long hours to accrue benefits for themselves, their families and the nation. One of the downsides of productive market economies is that too many comforts can make people too comfortable. An unearned sense of entitlement dulls initiative. That is not the case in China.

Encourage openness

Communication is more indirect in China. Companies generally adopt a Confucian-like order in the workplace, where everyone has a prescribed role. Respect for corporate hierarchy can add efficiency but stifle candour and creativity. Just because this traditional structure is in place doesn't mean people would prefer it, if offered the option of more autonomy. Some Chinese workers also have difficulty with the same ritualised interaction and opaqueness that can frustrate Westerners.

Recruit and educate

Rapidly growing Chinese companies face two overlapping personnel issues: finding qualified people for challenging jobs and educating them to think critically. Education systems reflect their societies. China traditionally has stressed rote education, preparing people to fit into a society where everyone has a role. To build societies around the primacy of the individual, western education is more likely to encourage people to ask questions, challenge received wisdom and work to achieve personal potential. Like most generalisations, this one is exaggerated. It's indisputable, however, that the sustained success of Chinese companies will require more workers with critical thinking skills.

TAKE AWAYS

品牌

Brand

Brand

Respect the competition

During the past 30 years China served as the world's factory. The arrangement enabled western consumers to improve their lives with more goods at lower prices. It also introduced more job opportunities to China, raising wages over time and reducing poverty. That stage of development is drawing to a close, as some western companies shift production to lower-cost economies and Chinese companies apply the knowledge learned as OEMs (Original Equipment Manufacturers) and ODMs (Original Design Manufacturers) to create and market their own branded merchandise. China is rebalancing from fast growth to more sustainable slower growth and from an economy driven by production for export to an economy driven by consumption at home. When building brands in China prepare to face experienced competitors.

Explore the country

Internet access has whet an appetite for brands in smaller cities, where competition is less heated than in the coastal metropolises. When considering cities in China, the word smaller is relative. More than 235 cities have populations over 500,000 compared with just 51 in 1980, around the start of economic reform. And the population of over 160 cities exceeds one million. Household income and home ownership is rising in many of these urban centres. Consumers tend to be more practical and less status driven than on the coast. What works for a brand in Shanghai may not work in Hohhot, the capital of Inner Mongolia (population 3 million). But it could be worth finding out what does work.

Mind the gap

Chinese brands face a credibility gap. Don't be fooled by it. They contend with several disadvantages when expanding abroad. First, most Chinese brands are relatively unknown outside of China. Second, fairly or not, "Brand China" often is associated with product quality and safety issues. Third, "Brand China" can also evoke social concerns, like factory working conditions. The main point about the gap, however, is that it's likely to narrow. The values of economic stability and shared prosperity articulated in the "Chinese Dream" will shape the notion of "Brand China." And based on how most developments happen in China, change should come quickly. The message for companies determined to develop a brand in China: Don't plan to compete against today's "Brand China" or you'll be well positioned for yesterday's market.

CHINA

AT A GLANCE

Key Facts and Figures

Economy

GDP

$4.522 trillion — 2008
$8.227 trillion — 2012

+82% over five years

GDP per Capita

$3,414 — 2000
$6,091 — 2010

+78%

Annual GDP growth over the past decade

Year	Growth
2003	10.0%
2004	10.1%
2005	11.3%
2006	12.7%
2007	14.2%
2008	9.6 %
2009	9.2%
2010	10.4%
2011	9.3%
2012	7.8%

In GDP, China is second only to the United States ($15.685 trillion GDP), which it is expected to surpass in less than a decade.

Savings Rate 53% (2011)

Chinese people are savers. The overall national savings rate is 53 per cent of GDP. In comparison, the savings rate for the United States is 12 per cent, the United Kingdom, 13 per cent; Brazil, 17 per cent; France, 18 per cent; Japan, 22 per cent; Germany, 24 per cent; and Russia, 30 per cent.

Foreign Direct Investment $253.5 billion (2012)

China leads the world, just ahead of the United States, in FDI, investments made by foreign entities acquiring an interest in local enterprises.

Communication

Mobile Phones — 1.2 billion
Internet Users — 591 million
Mobile Internet Users — 420 million

China leads in number of mobile phones, followed by India, the United States and Brazil.

Transportation

Airports — 507 (2013)
Railways — 86,000 km (53,438 mi)
Roads — 4.1 million km (2.5 million mi)

China is rapidly adding airports to accommodate burgeoning air traffic, but it currently ranks number 14 in the world, after Germany. The country is third in railways after the United States and Russia and second in roads, following the United States.

Consumers

People who believe brand matters 51.2% **Brand**

The importance of brand is growing. In just the three-year period between 2009 and 2011, the percentage of people throughout China who believe that brand matters and affects how others view them increased from 45.3 per cent to 51.2 per cent.

Sources: Grant Thornton International Business Report, The World Bank, National Bureau of Statistics of China, China Internet Network Information Center, The World Fact Book (CIA), CNRS-TGI

THE CHAIRMEN
AND THEIR
COMPANIES

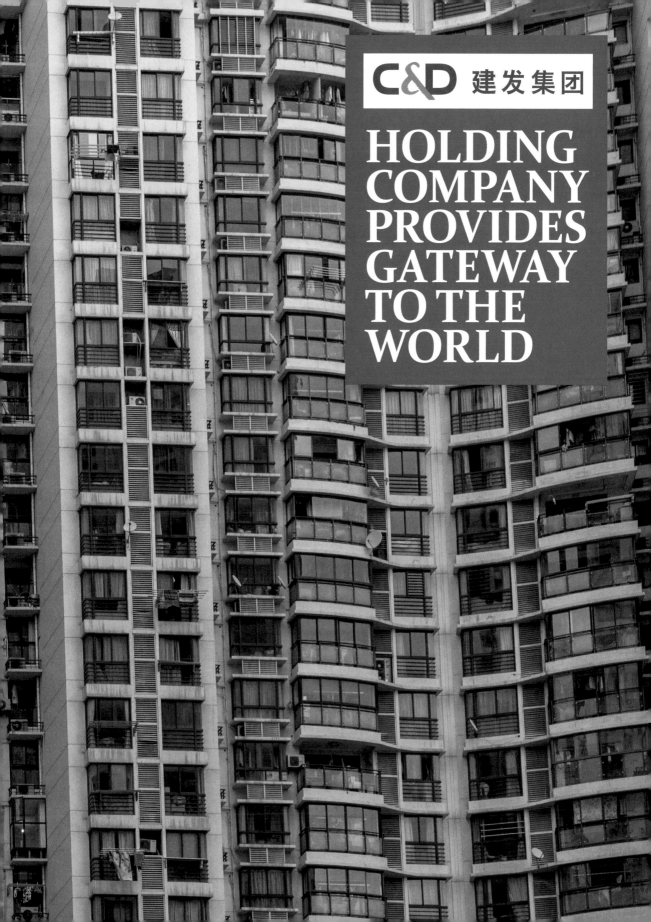

C&D 建发集团

HOLDING
COMPANY
PROVIDES
GATEWAY
TO THE
WORLD

Xiamen C&D Corporation, Ltd.

CHAIRWOMAN	WANG XIANRONG
INDUSTRY	DIVERSIFIED HOLDING COMPANY
OWNERSHIP	LOCAL SOE
SALES TURNOVER	(2012) RMB 94.1 BILLION ($15.4 BILLION)
HEADQUARTERS	XIAMEN
YEAR FORMED	1980

C&D is a holding company focussed on four broad businesses: supply chain logistics; real estate development; tourism and hotels; and conferences and exhibitions.

The company's supply chain businesses include shipbuilding and terminal operation, mining and the import and export of both industrial products and consumer products, including wine and cars. Its real estate holdings include commercial developments, such as the Xiamen International Conference and Exhibition Center.

Located along China's southeastern coast, Xiamen historically had been a trade gateway connecting China to the outside world. As Deng Xiaoping attempted to stimulate China's economy in the early 1980s, Xiamen was a logical location of a Special Economic Zone with more liberal commercial policies.

The government established Xiamen Construction and Development Corporation as one of China's many "window companies," a point of entry and exchange for international trading. This predecessor company subsequently was named Xiamen C&D Corporation, Ltd.

In 1998, Xiamen C&D Corporation, Ltd., established Xiamen C&D Inc., a subsidiary to focus on the supply chain and real estate development businesses. Xiamen C&D Inc. was listed on the Shanghai Stock Exchange in 1998. Xiamen C&D Corporation, Ltd. operates two other subsidiaries: Xiamen C&D Tourism and Hotels Inc. and Xiamen Conference and Exhibition Group Inc.

Workers at a C&D construction site in Xiamen.

建设

Construction

CONTEXT
INSIGHT
★

Home Ownership

Real estate investment will help stimulate shift from saving to spending

Private investment in real estate is a key element of the Chinese government effort to develop an economy driven more by domestic consumption than production and export.

The stimulus that real estate could provide is especially critical, given current saving and consumption patterns in China. In 2011, Chinese consumers saved 52 per cent of their annual income compared with 38 per cent in 2000, according to the China Statistical Yearbook. At the same time, the consumption rate declined to around 48 per cent from 62 per cent in 2000.

Shifting how people allocate their income, from saving to spending, requires government action to address the core societal reasons that influence this balance. People save in part because they lack confidence in current national programmes for covering basic needs, including healthcare, retirement and education.

The government also can stimulate spending with policies that encourage real estate development beyond the major cities. The development in lower tier cities is inevitable as Chinese and foreign companies expand into these areas, producing jobs and increasing affluence.

The price of an average home in Tier 1 and 2 cities increased to over RMB 5,791 per square meter in 2012 ($946), from RMB 2,063 ($337) per square meter in 1998, according to the National Bureau of Statistics of China. Meanwhile, in Tier 1 cities the price soared to an average of over RMB 15,261 ($2,492) and continues to rise.

Research and analysis by Millward Brown, a WPP company

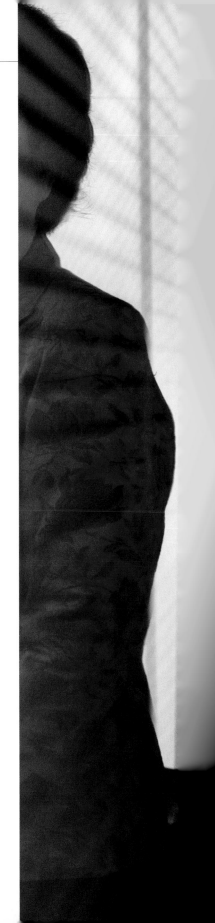

CHAIRWOMAN
WANG XIANRONG

Pioneer entrepreneur builds major enterprise

She now plans for more growth and succession

Chairwoman Wang Xianrong occupies an office in Xiamen, one of the country's initial Special Economic Zones.

It was in locations like this that the government of Deng Xiaoping opened China to permit foreign investment and the export of Chinese products to the West. Wang was among the first generation of entrepreneurial managers.

 "Back then we were searching for foreign trade so we had a lot of contact with foreign companies," she said. "We saw a different world long before State Owned Enterprises (SOEs) in the rest of China. We knew we were special and privileged to have that opportunity."

Wang graduated from Xiamen University with a degree in economics. She joined Xiamen C&D Corporation, Ltd., in 1984, as an accountant and went through two years of training in international economics and trade studies. Steady career advancement culminated with her appointment as chairwoman in 2007.

"The times have changed but the focus has not," said Wang. "We still are a window for the world and continue to attract steady growth and investment from overseas as well as from the interior of China."

About to retire, Wang delegates much responsibility to her trusted staff. Her goal now is to push company growth over RMB 100 billion ($16.5 billion) by 2015 and to facilitate the smooth transfer of leadership to her successor.

"I was talking to my only grandson the other day," she said. "I told him he must do what he loves and be happy. That is what I have done. I have followed my dreams. I just want him to be happy and do what he loves to do. But I also told him he must have principles and then let them guide every small thing he does."

IN HER OWN WORDS

Q&A with Chairwoman Wang Xianrong

PERSPECTIVE ON A CHINESE COMPANY

How do you make rapid decisions in a complex company?

We are agile. We are specialised in the many businesses we have and the people who run them deal with the day-to-day detail. I do not. I deal with the overview and the principles and policies we have. These principles and policies provide guidance for those operating our various businesses.

We are very clear about our business model. We manage the business by industry. We make macro-level adjustments to policy and the leaders in the business make the micro-level changes that are needed. We make very fast changes to manage our inventory and supply chain arrangements.

How do you choose the people to run the business?

I have only two criteria. First, can they delegate and make the team beneath them deliver the required outcomes? Second, what are their personal ethics? It is only when these two things are in balance that we will give people more responsibility.

How do you recruit the people you need at the highest levels?

It is not easy. This is an issue for businesses across China. It is very difficult to recruit the high level people. They may be good in the interview but then they do not perform well in the job.

So we prefer to develop our own people. We are just starting to use executive recruiters. Also, I have to admit that if we work with other companies and find good people, then we will hire them.

How do you ensure excellence in management succession?

Normally, local government will make these executive appointments to SOEs. But I do not agree with this approach. I believe the business must have the right people leading it to a sustainable future.

That means picking the right people and not simply a government appointed, ex-official who may not understand the business. I must convince the local government leaders to let us decide who should take over.

C&D apartment complex under construction in Xiamen.

KEEPING PACE
WITH RAPID CHANGE

How do you plan for the future?

From a company perspective, we live in uncertain times. We can no longer write a five-year plan easily. We can no longer write even an annual plan. We now have a quarterly plan, but we review it every month to ensure we are moving fast enough to capture the opportunities as they emerge. We need to think very carefully. The decisions we make each month could have impact 10-to-20 years in the future.

How has the global economic slow down impacted your business?

About 90 per cent of our business has been affected by the slow down. About 50 per cent of the business is supply chain related, so things like global steel and raw materials prices have hit construction costs hard. Pricing is so sensitive. We have to watch it every month.

What are your expectations for the next 12 months?

I am not too optimistic about the global economy, but there may be some regional variations. Real estate prices across Southeast Asia offer some opportunities, if you are careful. Also, depressed prices in North America and Europe offer more opportunities.

Africa is good but the volumes are not there even though the rates of growth are. We have to be careful and agile. Asia has the best opportunities. That is where I am most hopeful. The countries around China are interesting. The people in Asia have the energy and drive to do something and they have the ambition to achieve it, too.

A Shanghai skyline suggests the intensity of real estate development and the rapid rise in home ownership.

Workers select building materials.

> " From a company perspective, we live in uncertain times. We can no longer write a five-year plan easily. We can no longer write even an annual plan. "

CHINA AND THE WEST

What's the key difference between the Chinese and western view of business?

In the West, everything in business is black and white. But in China it is about balance. To find the middle way, to achieve balance, the win-win situation in everything we do. To find the middle way for all is a good thing. We try to find a way for us to communicate how we can do things for the benefit of all.

To succeed in China, western people need to understand this approach. It's possible for Westerners to learn it. I am a board director at a local investment bank and I have a fellow director who is an American. Over the years, he has learned more and now he will consult me for my opinion before he speaks on an important matter. He is learning the Chinese ways. To draw back and be reflective before acting is not bad.

What do western people most need to understand about China?

The leaders of businesses in China have a lot of heart for what they do. The Chinese people will put their energy and efforts into what they do. It is not just for the money. They want to realise their dreams and to do something valuable for China.

There are opportunities everywhere. There are challenges, of course and the key challenge is the changing society in which we live. We need to influence that environment. But we are resilient and diligent and we will achieve what we set out to do.

What is China's main challenge now?

The local government faces important challenges. How will it continue to lead this convergence with capitalism? How will it continue to encourage this spirit in the people? We need the government to have the commitment to do the good things. We need to see how it can really help the people to succeed. That is the challenge for China now.

How do you think China will meet these challenges?

My view is the middle way, neither pessimistic nor optimistic. I am optimistic by temperament. I arrive at the middle way by being pessimistic about the big issues that face China right now. Further reforms are necessary. We have had fast growth in China from the great opening up, but now we have less growth. I am not sure that the new leadership has the appetite for further reforms, but we need them. The national leaders need to push things forward. There are many problems and they are not easy to solve.

> " In the West, everything in business is black and white. But in China it is about balance. To find the middle way, to achieve balance, the win-win situation in everything we do. "

Lunch break near a C&D development.

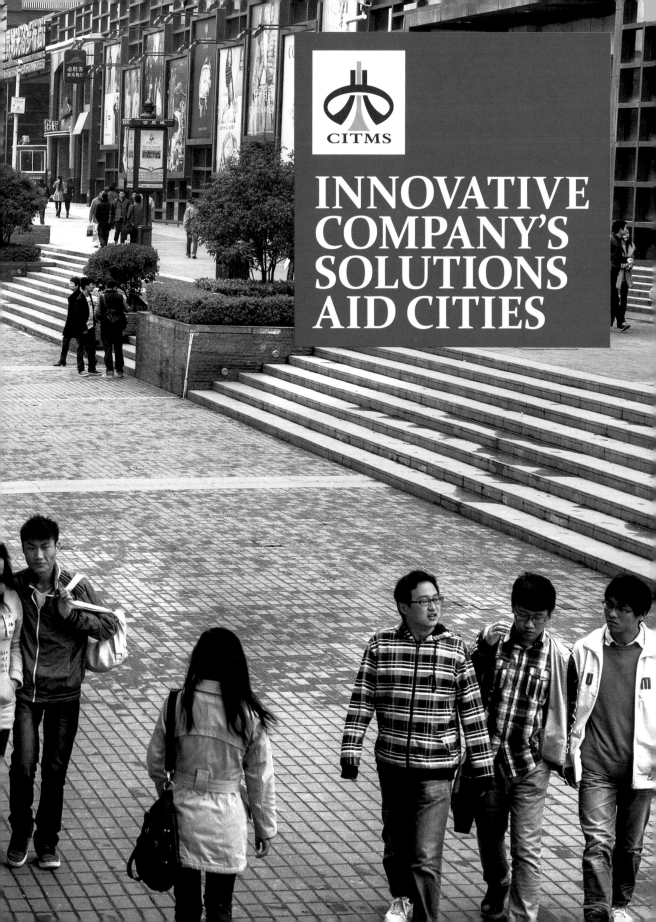

INNOVATIVE COMPANY'S SOLUTIONS AID CITIES

CITMS

City Intelligent Transport Management Systems

科技

Technology

PRESIDENT	WANG KAIXUE
INDUSTRY	TRANSPORTATION TECHNOLOGY
OWNERSHIP	PRIVATE
SALES (2012)	RMB 63.5 MILLION ($10.4 MILLION)
HEADQUARTERS	WUHAN
YEAR FORMED	2007

CITMS develops and manages intelligent transportation technology surveillance systems used by metropolitan authorities for automated traffic control and public safety.

President Wang

Examples of the company's products include systems for operating traffic lights and for monitoring parking, with the ability to detect and record violations. The company invests 6-to-7 per cent of annual income in research and development to produce innovations and protect its competitive advantage.

The largest provider of intelligent transportation technology solutions in Hubei Province, in Central China, CITMS has expanded to neighbouring Henan, Jiujiang and Jiangxi Provinces as well as to the coastal cities of Shenzhen and Tianjin.

A CITMS surveillance camera monitors a Wuhan street.

Traffic

Car ownership, traffic congestion reaching lower tier cities

Around 120 million privately owned cars clogged China's roads at the end of 2012. The number is expected to pass 200 million by 2020. And the further potential is enormous considering that the rate of car ownership in China is 54 cars per 1,000 individuals, less than half of the ownership average worldwide.

This explosive increase in cars has produced a related indicator of growing affluence—traffic congestion, especially in the Tier 1 cities. The government responses include municipal-level restrictions on automobile private ownership and efforts to improve traffic flow. Companies like CITMS have provided technological solutions.

Now primarily a phenomenon of Tier 1 cities, car ownership and the need to manage traffic will shift to lower tier cities where the market potential is greatest. Car sales increased by less than 10 per cent in Tier 1 cities in 2012, according to the China Automobile Dealers Association. But in Tier 2 and 3 cities, where car ownership is low, sales grew by 131 per cent. In Changsha, the capital of Hunan province, for example, only 12 per cent of the population own cars.

Research and analysis by Millward Brown, a WPP company

PRESIDENT
WANG KAIXUE

Professor leaves teaching and builds successful business

His traffic control systems improve cities

Wang Kaixue expected to teach.

After graduating from Wuhan University as a mechanical engineer, in 1986, he joined the faculty and stayed for several years building a career in academia.

His plans changed in 1992, the year of Deng Xiaoping's famous Southern Tour to publicise the success of China's Special Economic Zones and solidify support for a more open economy. Wang, like many others, recognised an opportunity.

"I had a strong feeling that I need to change my life and do something that I wanted to do and could do," said Wang. "The opening in Shenzhen provided a platform for people with a certain level of technical know-how, a sense of social responsibility and vision. Many of us who went into business then are now business leaders in various sectors. We call these people, the "Generation of '92."

Wang worked in Shenzhen for over a decade, until 2005, when he spent a year in Beijing before returning to Wuhan, where government action again influenced his career choice. Vehicle traffic was so bad, the government decided to intervene by adding more police officers.

Traffic flow might improve, Wang agreed, but only when officers were present, which would not be 24/7. Without officers, traffic flow again would deteriorate. Wang presented a technological solution, an electronic system to monitor traffic continuously.

The government offered financial support, which Wang rejected, offering instead to invest RMB 5 million ($815,000) of company funds to build an intelligent transportation monitoring system.

"At the time, I saw this purely from a financial and business perspective," Wang said. "The result, seeing the positive impact on the city, changed my thinking. I feel that it is part of the responsibility of enterprises to leverage their business in providing solutions to social problems."

President Wang near an office of the Wuhan police, a CITMS client.

66
I feel that
it is part of the
responsibility of
enterprises to leverage
their business in
providing solutions
to social problems. 99

IN HIS OWN WORDS

Q&A with President Wang Kaixue

PERSPECTIVE ON A CHINESE COMPANY

What motivated you to build a business?

Originally, my colleagues and I thought about our company from a financial and business perspective. Later developments changed our thinking. And we realised that what we do is closely related to people's lives and wellbeing. When we created an electronic system for solving the traffic situation in Wuhan, I noticed that the entire city seemed more orderly. It was a big surprise to us at the time, the fact that the investment from a company can actually change something fundamental. This is another reason why the business grew so quickly. We understood more about the impact we could have.

Is your story representative of other entrepreneurs?

When the government declared the success of Special Economic Zones, like Shenzhen, in 1992, it signalled opportunity for people who had a certain level of technical know-how, social responsibility, conviction and vision. I'm describing the "Generation of '92" that went into business after leaving positions as government officials, teachers or business leaders of SOEs.

China's economic and political climate provided a relatively free environment for this group of people and their businesses to flourish. The "Generation of '92" managed to grab this opportunity. But after a period of wealth accumulation, these individuals start to ask, "Now I have money, what would I like to do with it?" They started to build and run their businesses not just as machines for making money, but also as tools to benefit society.

To what do you attribute the success of your company?

The reason for our success is opportune timing. The business universe is in alignment. In our case, the industry is growing rapidly, the technology sector is relatively behind here in central China, compared with the coast, government is providing leadership and our business team is strong and focussed.

Heavy traffic clogs Shanghai road.

> " The reason for our success is opportune timing. The business universe is in alignment. The industry is growing rapidly. "

KEEPING PACE WITH RAPID CHANGE

How do you manage the risk and speed of growth?

We have discussed this topic a lot. When an enterprise develops to a certain size, the management team feels the desire to grow bigger. This attitude is especially strong in new, developing businesses. But you soon realise that in comparing the size of the company to its internal health, its health far outweighs the size in importance.

In fact, we have already encountered this problem of whether rapid growth is supported by the systems of the business. So now we are much more focussed on the health of the business, building up the corporate culture and the management team. With both these elements in place we can better handle rapid growth.

Your focus is smart technology, so where do you find your smart people?

The Chinese are all very smart. More seriously, it's important to guarantee a secure future for these smart people. And it's important to provide a platform where they can demonstrate their talent. We ask people if they want to join us on particular projects. After focusing for a few years in one industry, they become expert. We had about six people in 2007, now we have about 200. This is all part of building the business, having your people grow with your business.

Where do you look for management expertise?

Strictly speaking, my understanding of management is a recent thing. In 2007, I spent a year in Wuhan University and attended lectures on management. That year had a profound effect on me. It taught me what modern business management really means. Our business is mostly about providing comprehensive solutions. It requires particular team-building skills.

People who want to further themselves must pay attention to the wealth of knowledge left behind by the previous generations. There is a saying: "Clever people learn from other people's mistakes." Looking at this idea another way, clever people find the mistakes in other people's experiences. I think studying is of utmost importance for improving oneself and the whole management team. I am completing an MBA at Wuhan University now.

> 66
> We are much more focussed on the health of the business, building up the corporate culture and the management team. With both these elements in place we can better handle rapid growth. 99

Traffic converges in Wuhan.

天時地利人和
[Opportune]

In the English translation of President Wang's remarks he ascribes the success of CITMS in part to opportune timing. One English word does not adequately convey the nuances embedded in the phrase he used: 天时地利人和. The first two historical sources for 天时地利人, almost 2,500 old, are found in the writings of the military strategist Sun Bin and Meng Zi, a philosopher. They describe the best strategic moment to strike: When the weather is favourable 天时, the environment is favourable 地利 and the desires of the people are united 人和.

CHINA AND THE WEST

How do you see China fitting into the global marketplace?

Having travelled to many places in the world, I think the Chinese are especially industrious and kind and have a strong spirit for teamwork. The Chinese are also keen to learn and very strong at creating things.

We hope that we can combine these characteristics with technology from the West, to help advance positive change in China. We also want to share what the Chinese create with the rest of the world with an open attitude and for the world to have an open attitude towards China.

Do you have international ambitions?

We would like to become an influential and exceptional company in China in the next five years. In the past, we had singular projects aimed only locally, but in 2011 we started going into the rest of China, including Tianjin, in the north; Henan Province, in central China; Shenzhen, on the southern coast; Jiujiang in Jiangxi province and Wuhu in Hubei province.

So we are already in other parts of China. As to whether we will expand overseas, I don't have a plan for this at the moment. As the Chinese economy develops and when the natural expansion and growth of the company reaches that level, I'm sure there will be overseas opportunities.

Are Chinese and western social responsibility comparable?

In China, if businesses really take their social responsibility seriously, then the government will distribute more resources and opportunities to them. Companies that are big and successful are closely related to the leadership and direction of the government. It is a key ingredient for the growth of these companies in China.

In this sense, the "Generation of '92" is quite different from entrepreneurs in the West. In China, where the central government has ultimate control of the economy, there is a close relationship between the demands coming from the government and the macro environment and the resources, attitude and vision of these businesses.

*Pedestrians pass a CITMS
surveillance camera in Wuhan.*

> " In China, if businesses really take their social responsibility seriously, then the government will distribute more resources and opportunities to them. "

VEHICLE MAKER BUILDS BRAND IN CHINA, OTHER FAST GROWING MARKETS

Beiqi Foton Motor Company, Ltd.

汽车

Car
Manufacturing

VICE PRESIDENT	GONG YUEQIONG
INDUSTRY	MOTOR VEHICLES
OWNERSHIP	STATE HOLDING ENTERPRISE
SALES (2012)	RMB 41 BILLION ($6.7 BILLION)*
HEADQUARTERS	BEIJING
YEAR FORMED	1996

Foton is China's leading manufacturer of commercial motor vehicles, including buses and trucks. The company also produces several models of passenger cars, SUVs and vans.

Although Foton trades mostly in China, it also distributes internationally, primarily in India, Africa and other fast growing markets. Along with the Foton brand, the company offers several sub-brands, including Auman, AUV, Aumark, Forland and MP-X.

Based in Beijing, Foton operates research and development centres in China as well as in Japan and Germany. It has assembly plants located throughout China and in Russia, Pakistan, Vietnam and India, with another planned for Mexico.

A joint venture with Germany's Daimler provides Foton with additional technical expertise and co-branding opportunities. Foton employs almost 38,000 people. It is a publicly traded company on the Shanghai Stock Exchange. The Chinese government holds a minority stake.

Foton trucks at work site.

* Does not include joint ventures.

CONTEXT INSIGHT

★

Car Manufacturing

Rapid growth presents opportunities and challenges for China's car brands

The production and sales of Chinese cars reached 19.3 million units in 2012, making China the world's largest auto market for the fourth consecutive year. In second place, the US produced just over 10 million units. The disparity indicates China's importance as a generator of sales and profit for foreign companies

China's car manufacturing business has grown at a rapid and steady pace since the country's accession to the World Trade Organisation (WTO) in 2001. Similarly China's international auto trade has increased evenly except for a slowdown during the 2009 global financial crisis.

The country imported just over one million units and exported slightly more, during 2012. Chinese cars are especially accepted in developing markets, where 62 per cent of consumers are willing to consider a Chinese car brand compared with 55 per cent in developed markets, according to the Millward Brown Going Global Study 2011. The top countries for export include Algeria, Brazil, Iraq, Russia, Iran and Chile.

In tapping the great domestic and international potential, Chinese car brands face several challenges. When selling cars at home they need to confront the continuing Chinese preference for foreign brands, especially for luxury passenger cars. For the export market, the carmakers need to strengthen the image of "Brand China."

"Brand China" is characterised as innocent, friendly, kind and caring, based on analysis powered by WPP's BrandZ™ brand analytic database. As the Chinese brands seek greater acceptance, both at home and abroad, the nation will need to strengthen the "Brand China" personality with other characteristics, such as being perceived as trustworthy and wise and offering quality. To compete in the luxury car sector the brands will need to strengthen their emotional appeal and badge status.

Research and analysis by Millward Brown, a WPP company

VICE PRESIDENT
GONG YUEQIONG

> 66 It's important to provide value to everyone engaged in the enterprise, which includes shareholders, but also corporate partners and staff. 99

Younger generation manager targets international growth

Sees corporate success tied to personal fitness

Gong Yueqiong represents China's younger generation of professional managers.

He joined Foton immediately after university, in 1998, as one of the motor vehicle company's first trainees. He became vice president, finance, in 2011.

Foton prepared Gong for corporate leadership by exposing him to departments across the entire organisation. To help Gong understand global opportunities and broaden his industry knowledge, Foton involved him with its international partner companies, including Toyota, General Motors and Tata.

"It's most important to have a learning heart and to be open to new things. In this way you help the company and also expand your own capabilities."

Along with finance, Gong's responsibilities today include mergers and acquisitions. Among his specific business challenges are finding capital for investment in technology and international expansion, particularly to developing markets, where Gong sees the greatest opportunity.

While financial performance—market share, revenue and profit—remains the most important indicator of corporate success for Gong, he also stresses the need to be a responsible corporate citizen.

"It's critical to respect the environment. And it's important to provide value to everyone engaged in the enterprise, which includes shareholders, but also corporate partners and staff."

Achieving corporate success depends in part on the personal health and fitness of individual leaders, Gong believes. "It's a challenge after age 40, particularly in China where doing business involves drinking," he joked. "But it's vital to exercise, to keep in good physical shape and also to maintain a good balance of work and family."

Vice President Gong with trucks that just arrived from the factory.

IN HIS OWN WORDS

问答
Q&A

Q&A with Vice President Gong Yueqiong

PERSPECTIVE ON A CHINESE COMPANY

What is your vision for the Foton brand?

We are both optimistic and realistic. We believe that it's possible for Chinese companies to build strong brands. But it will take more than a decade to have the kind of global brands that some western companies built over a century. We must learn everything about brand building and delivering quality and a good customer experience. We can't be the best in the world right now, but we can strive to be the international standard for mid-range products. We can be a leader in this sector.

Will you acquire established brands or build the Foton brand?

The idea of developing and exporting an independent Chinese brand is a great dream. But it takes time. In the early stages of development, we leveraged the appeal of our fast growing market to attract western brands that entered into joint ventures and shared their technology. Now we're in a later stage. And our challenge is not simply to acquire western brands, but to build our own Chinese brands. Chinese consumers are now more sophisticated and that's what they're looking for.

Every brand has a heart, what is the heart of the Foton brand?

This is a good but difficult question that every business must be able to answer. The heart of the Foton brand is that we want to deliver a sense of innovation and a spirit for progress. And that's how we want people to see us.

How much time does Foton's top management spend thinking about the brand?

The development of the Foton brand is our top priority and we spend a lot of time on it. We think both domestically and also about what the image of the Foton brand will be globally. We used to think of brand as only communication. But we understand brand differently now. It's embedded in our strategy and execution, into everything that we do.

Display of Foton logo and miniature vehicles in Vice President Gong's office.

66
We believe that
it's possible for Chinese
companies to build strong
brands. But it will take
more than a decade
to have the kind
of global brands
that some western
companies built
over a century. 99

KEEPING PACE WITH RAPID CHANGE

What impact has Foton had on China?

We are a listed company. The government is a minor shareholder, so we actually developed from the market economy. We are innovative. We are an example of the potential strength of a Chinese company. Most of our customers are small businesses that use our products to help create their own wealth. Many Chinese companies learn from us and we see ourselves as a model of Chinese businesses in the future.

What will growth be like in China?

We will continue to enjoy strong results in China. But China's rate of economic expansion will slow somewhat. It will be relatively strong, but not the double-digit growth that we had experienced.

Where are the opportunities?

Industry growth, which began in Europe and the US, shifted during the past few decades to Asia, first to Japan and then Korea. Now it's shifting to China and developing markets. Foton is well positioned to meet consumer needs in these new markets. Brazil, India and Russia are the next areas for growth.

Given these changing dynamics, what are the key challenges for growth?

First, we must continue to advance technologically so that we can develop quality cars, but with the relatively low operating costs that make us competitive. And as demand booms in Brazil, India and Russia we need to be there. Second, we need capital. In general, Chinese auto companies don't have sufficient access to capital to make the large investment required for international expansion at the level that's required to fully realise this opportunity.

Rapid growth can create quality problems, what's Foton's attitude toward recalls?

A car company should be proactive both in addressing any product problem and in communicating to customers. The structure and attitude of a management team will influence these decisions. It's important to view these problems from a long-term perspective. The cost of fixing a problem is a factor, but it must be considered in the context of the impact on the brand, which can be great if a company doesn't act correctly.

Foton leads the Chinese market in commercial vehicle sales.

> " We must continue to advance technologically so that we can develop quality cars, but with the relatively low operating costs that make us competitive. "

CHINA AND THE WEST

How do you see China's place—and its future—in the global car industry?

China is 10 years behind the European and American car industries. India is 20 years behind. These differences in technical development are also true from management and strategy perspectives. The management style of the European and American companies is modernised and systemised and their approach to strategy is mature and perfected.

In this context, what are Foton's competitive strengths?

We may not be able to compete with Europe or America yet technologically, but we have the know-how to create a good car at an affordable price. We can do that better than Brazil, India and Russia. And we have tremendous domestic demand, both for commercial vehicles and passenger cars. We are the market share leader in commercial vehicles in China for the eleventh consecutive year.

How do the Chinese and Indian companies compare?

The Chinese businesses are optimistic and confident about the future. But they don't anticipate and plan enough strategically. The Indian car companies tend to be closer to the European and American companies in management style. But they're not as competitively successful as the Chinese companies

How do you anticipate competing in Russia, which has its own auto industry?

We see a mismatch between the quality expectations of Russian consumers and the production capabilities of the Russian car industry. We need to find ways to invest in Russia that enable us to establish a business despite any trade barriers.

How will China's image affect Foton's global expansion?

The country's image will impact the level of investment we receive. China will need to change over the next 10 years so that we are accepted globally and can market our products. Our partners will need to feel that doing business with China is no more difficult than doing business in the West. The government will need to continue addressing challenges, such as narrowing the gap between rich and poor people.

> 66
> China will need to change over the next 10 years so that we are accepted globally and can market our products. 99

The Foton brand on the streets of Beijing.

福星惠誉
FUXINGHUIYU

HOME OWNERSHIP BOOM DRIVES GROWTH FOR REAL ESTATE DEVELOPER

Fuxing Huiyu Real Estate Company, Ltd.

CEO	HU SHUOSHAN
INDUSTRY	REAL ESTATE DEVELOPMENT
OWNERSHIP	LISTED COMPANY
SALES (2012)	RMB 4.3 BILLION ($701.5 MILLION)
HEADQUARTERS	WUHAN
YEAR FORMED	2001

Fuxing Huiyu develops high-end real estate, primarily in Wuhan but also in Hainan and Beijing, with plans to move into lower tier markets as part of its aspiration to become a leading national company.

Its establishment, in 2001, signalled the diversification of its parent holding company, Hubei Fuxing Science and Technology Company, Ltd. With significant assets and a strong balance sheet the company sought new business opportunities following its listing on the Shenzhen Stock Exchange in 1999.

The listing coincided with the Chinese government's reform of housing, from a policy based on government subsidy to one driven by private home ownership. Recognising a chance to enter into a potentially fast-growth industry, Hubei Fuxing management formed Fuxing Huiyu Real Estate Company, Ltd.

As Fuxing Huiyu expands its real estate holdings, the company also is focussed on strengthening its operations by improvement of the management systems, corporate governance and recruitment and retention mechanisms.

The Fuxing Huiyu brand appears at the top of the round building on the right, in Wuhan.

房地产

Real Estate

CONTEXT
INSIGHT
★

Home Ownership

Home ownership touches spectrum of basic needs

The notion of home ownership is deeply embedded in Chinese culture.

Ownership is a key priority because it touches many needs that can be arranged on a hierarchical pyramid, starting with the functional on the bottom and ending with the emotional at the top.

In ascending order, the levels of this pyramid include: (1) physical protection and living space; (2) comfort and a legacy for children; (3) enjoyment and family life; and (4) a symbol of accomplishment and "face." Face is a combination of self-esteem and public respect or stature. It is a fundamental concept in a society that values order and connects personal dignity to how well one performs his or her role.

Rising affluence has accelerated home ownership and influenced the way people purchase homes, the kinds of dwellings they prefer, the prices they pay and the debt they're willing to assume. But it has not altered the centrality of the home and its connection to the Chinese deep attachment to the land and reverence for family.

HOME OWNERSHIP AND CULTURAL VALUES

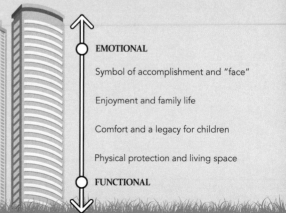

EMOTIONAL

Symbol of accomplishment and "face"

Enjoyment and family life

Comfort and a legacy for children

Physical protection and living space

FUNCTIONAL

Home ownership is important in China for both practical and cultural reasons.

Source: Millward Brown, a WPP company

CEO
HU SHUOSHAN

Youthful CEO drives growth of young company

Values connect welfare of business, community and country

When Fuxing Huiyu named Hu Shuoshan Chief Financial Officer, around 10 years ago, he was 26, the youngest CFO of any of China's publicly listed companies.

Hu joined Hubei Fuxing Science and Technology Company, Ltd., as an accountant, in 1996, directly from university. He moved to Fuxing Huiyu Real Estate Ltd. when the real estate subsidiary was listed in 1999.

Hu's rapid rise reflects his abilities and determination, but also the influence of his mentor, the founder and chairman of Fuxing Huayi, Tan Guoyan. Like other Chinese entrepreneurs, his vision and personality have shaped the company he started and the careers of its employees.

"The chairman really believed in me," said Hu. "He has had an influence on shaping my personality and building my values. Following the traditional Chinese culture, I will use the rest of my life to pay back this trust."

Hu became Fuxing Huiyu CEO in 2012, a promotion that he describes as a transition in focus from the part to the whole, from tactics to strategy and from implementation to management. He now balances the risk management mentality of his financial training with the need to grow the business.

"My values lie in making the company bigger and better."

He expressed similar feelings about his commitment to Wuhan, which Hu considers his hometown. He believes that career success requires dedication, not just to an industry, but also to the wellbeing of one's community and country.

"Simply put," said Hu, "love is the energy driving contribution, productivity and creativity."

CEO Hu in front of one of his company's properties in Wuhan.

66

Simply put,
love is the
energy driving
contribution,
productivity
and creativity.

99

IN HIS OWN WORDS

问答

Q&A

Q&A with Chief Executive Hu Shuoshan

PERSPECTIVE ON A CHINESE COMPANY

What philosophy guides your approach to business?

There is a saying that establishes priorities: "First be a person. Then do things." In this case, the words "be" and "do" are expressed with the same Chinese character. These other aphorisms also contain meaning. "Every little thing for the client is a big thing for us." Also, "The creation of value is the foundation of future success." And, "Sharing value to win together in the future." These guiding thoughts can be distilled to four key principles for building and operating a successful business: being honest, sharing the value, acting responsibly and winning together.

What is required of a CEO to create a great company?

CEOs must do two things well: manage risk and create value. For a company to grow, risk management is the first step. After this, you will be able to realise rapid growth. Of course, you can't let risk management get in the way of growth. It is a means for enabling growth. There is risk in every opportunity and opportunity in every risk. To create value, the CEO needs to find appropriate strategies to manage this balance, meet shareholder profit goals and demonstrate social responsibility.

Do you agree with those who say the CEO job is a lonely one?

In traditional Chinese culture that idea would be expressed as "You will feel cold in a high place." Or you are in a dangerous and precarious place being in a high position. I don't think that way. And, there is a view in China which comes from Sun Tzu, in *The Art of War*, which also contradicts this idea. It's based on the teachings of the philosopher Meng Zi, also from over 2,000 years ago.

First, if a leader has justice or enlightenment on his side and can implement a good strategy and management system, then staff would approve and support him. Second, you need many soldiers and generals, in other words, a lot of talented people to implement the plan. If you can have so many talented good people who support you and respect you, how can you possibly be lonely?

New construction reflects the growing demand for home ownership.

NUANCE
INSIGHT

做人，做事
[Be, Do]

The words be and do are each comprised of two characters. The first character 做 is identical for both words, implying an intrinsic connection between being and doing. One philosophical interpretation is that the essence of each individual is revealed only through action or interaction.

" For a company to grow, risk management is the first step. After this, you will be able to realise rapid growth. "

KEEPING PACE WITH RAPID CHANGE

How are you preparing the company to grow for many decades?

There are short-term, mid-term and long-term considerations when it comes to risk management. For short- to mid-term, we can build financial models for controlling risk. The long-term balance includes the diversification of product, business and format. There are many rules, targets and principles for these models that enable you to find the best balance between risk and opportunity.

How do you personally continue to learn, keep motivated and get inspired?

I have been studying continuously since receiving my degree and starting my career. I joined the business with a Bachelor's degree, in 1996. Five years later, in 2001, I did an MBA in Wuhan University. In 2011, I went to Huazhong University of Science and Technology for a Ph.D. in macro management. I am a visiting scholar to Hong Kong University.

The importance of studying is something I have felt very deeply throughout my career. Studying not only helps you with specific problems encountered in your work, it also improves thinking and problem solving. Study broadens your specialised knowledge and opens your vision and makes your thinking more comprehensive.

Does the position of CEO help you keep informed?

As CEO I have more and more friends that I truly admire and respect. I also have more people and more opinions to consult from a larger field. Now, many famous economists, specialists in management and successful entrepreneurs have become my friends. There are many ways for us to interact and learn from each other.

They can help me work through things that I can't understand. When I am stuck with something, by spending time with these people I can work it out and act with confidence. That's why I think being CEO gives you a better platform. It just depends how you take hold of this opportunity and make the best of it to make your work more simple, enjoyable, productive and valuable.

High-density developments serve both commercial and residential customers.

> " For short- to mid-term, we can build financial models for controlling risk. The long-term balance includes the diversification of product, business and format. "

CHINA AND THE WEST

What motivates Chinese business people?

On a recent visit to the University of Management in Singapore, the dean asked a group of us Chinese entrepreneurs this multiple choice question: How should Chinese entrepreneurs see their business: (a) As their child; (b) As their career; (c) As a commodity? Most people answered (a). I chose (b). No one chose option (c).

These responses reflect traditional Chinese values. They highlight the cultural difference between the West  and the East. Why did I choose (b)? I see the business as the platform where I will work hard in my life. A board director said something important: The value of Chinese entrepreneurs is seen through the longevity of their business. Perhaps the idea is not correct from a theoretical point of view, but I admire it.

How do individuals in a company differ in motivation?

I think it depends on your role in the organisation. From the perspective of the staff, the company probably divides into staff, management and shareholders. The management and shareholders think about creating the right kind of culture in which staff will want to participate and create value and build the company.

For a leader of a company, or a shareholder, feelings towards the company would be of the highest level. This is because their reputations, as well as their financial gain and loss, is directly linked with the success of the company. They are responsible for sustaining the long-term health of the company. Showing personal achievement is also important for middle management. The ordinary staff sees a job perhaps as a learning experience, but mostly it is a way to earn a living.

What advice do you have for western business people?

There needs to be an integration of western and Chinese cultures. China and the West differ in many areas, which is very normal and understandable. However, I hope western people will look at eastern culture in a rational and reasonable way.

Fuxing Huiyu construction just outside Wuhan.

> " China and the West differ in many areas, which is very normal and understandable. However, I hope western people will look at eastern culture in a rational and reasonable way. "

HOTEL BRAND EXPANDING THROUGHOUT CHINA, NOW LOOKS ABROAD FOR GROWTH

Home Inns & Hotels Management Inc.

CEO	DAVID SUN
INDUSTRY	HOTELS
OWNERSHIP	LISTED COMPANY
SALES (2012)	RMB 5.4 BILLION ($869.3 MILLION)
HEADQUARTERS	SHANGHAI
YEAR FORMED	2002

China's fastest-growing hotel brand, Home Inns operates locations throughout China with a brand proposition centred on providing consistent quality and comfort in convenient locations at an affordable price.

The company operates hotels under three brands: Home Inns, Motel 168 and Yitel. Home Inns, the original and largest brand and Motel 168, acquired in 2011, target budget travellers. Yitel is positioned for the mid- and up-market segments.

The chain grew rapidly, from 10 hotels in four cities in 2003, to 1,772 hotels in 253 cities at the end of 2012. The economy hotels range in size from 80-to-160 rooms and are situated in locations that draw both business and vacation guests. Almost 12 million individuals belonged to the company's loyalty programme at the end of 2012.

The owners of Ctrip, the successful online travel site, co-founded Home Inns in 2002. Home Inns & Hotels Management Inc. is incorporated in the Cayman Islands. The company completed a public offering in 2006 and is listed on the NASDAQ exchange.

Check-in at a Shanghai Home Inn.

旅行

Travel

Hotel Industry

Growing demand drives hotel industry expansion and brand consolidation

The value of China's hotel industry totalled $44 billion in 2012, with 2.5 million rooms. This result represents four hotel rooms per 1,000 individuals, a relatively low penetration rate compared with 10-to-20 hotel rooms per 1,000 individuals in more developed markets.

In a country of more than 1.3 billion people, this disparity represents enormous growth potential for the hotel industry and the national economy. Many Chinese policy makers see the travel industry as a key engine driving domestic consumption and the shift away from a manufacturing-driven economy. In the first quarter of 2013, for the first time, China's services sector exceeded its industrial sector in share of GDP.

Driven both by growing tourism and expanding business needs, the most explosive hotel industry expansion is expected in Tier 2 and 3 cities, with the greatest proportion of this activity concentrated in the budget and mid-level market segments. Both foreign and domestic brands are competing for this opportunity.

The Chinese brands are experiencing a period of consolidation, especially at the budget level, as illustrated by Home Inns' acquisitions of eJia Express, Motor 168 and Top Star Hotels. The more fragmented mid-level segment is likely to face consolidation pressure now, as budget operators expand into this segment.

The entrance of international players will also accelerate this consolidation. Global brands such as Marriott, Starwood, InterContinental and Accor had more than 400 new hotels in some stage of development during 2013. The increased presence of global players will intensify efforts to build brand loyalty. Both Chinese and foreign brands are likely to emphasise loyalty programmes.

Chinese customers give brand high consideration when choosing hotels, based on the expectation that brand promises quality and service. When travelling abroad, Chinese travellers tend to select familiar brands. Construction of the first Chinese brand five star hotel outside of China is planned for London, developed by Dalian Wanda Group, a Chinese real estate company.

Research and analysis by Millward Brown, a WPP company

CEO
DAVID SUN

A former retailer develops fastest-growing hotel chain

Still finds time for mahjong with his grandmother

No one is more surprised than David Sun that he's now head of China's fastest-growing hotel brand.

His parents, both doctors, expected Sun to follow their example. He received a bachelor's degree from Shanghai Medical University. But when he graduated, in the late 1980s, China was beginning to open to a world that he wanted to see.

With limited funds from his parents, Sun went to Australia and studied marketing in Melbourne, earning money with part-time employment at Woolworths, the Australian supermarket. He remained in Australia after graduation, spending four years working on shopping mall development.

When Sun returned home, in 1992, China was a changed country. Economic growth was strong. The business opportunities and vibrant social life appealed to the young man. He spent 12 years in retail, the last four years with a young Chinese super centre company called Lotus, where he learned the basics: merchandising, advertising and marketing.

He then joined the marketing department of B&Q, the UK-based international home improvement retailer, which entered China in 1999. The experience helped Sun think strategically and sharpened his appreciation of the contrast between Chinese and western business attitudes.

"When I joined B&Q, I gave my schedule for the month and my manager, who was British, asked, 'Why did you put Saturday and Sunday on that?'" Sun recalled. "The question surprised me because when I worked at Lotus, you thought of work as seven days a week, 24-hours a day."

The lesson about work-life balance still guides Sun. He also benefited from the autonomy

B&Q granted him. While B&Q shared its global experience, the company relied on its Chinese executives to adapt the DIY concept for the local market.

"I learned important lessons about execution and hard work from Chinese companies. But B&Q taught me how to plan and take initiative."

The decision to leave B&Q was difficult and unexpected. The owners of Home Inns, also the founders of Ctrip, the successful online travel site, shared their ambitious vision with Sun and tried to recruit him. The company, only two years old with 18 locations, planned to become the largest mid-priced hotel chain in China, if not the world.

They wanted a retailer to run the business. Sun rejected them three times, arguing that as a retailer he knew little about the hospitality industry. Then, while on vacation in Hawaii, he noticed the popularity of mid-priced hotel chains and understood the opportunity.

"The Home Inns people had looked at other hotel chains in China," said Sun. "No manager had experience with even hundreds of hotels and they wanted to open thousands." Today, 10 years later, Sun oversees 2,000 hotels in 270 Chinese cities. But the lesson about work-life balance learned at B&Q still guides him.

"Every Chinese New Year, for a week to 10 days, I visit around 100 hotels to say hello and celebrate the holidays with the staff." Sun added, "Every two weeks I visit my 99-year-old grandmother and maybe play some mahjong. When she asks me, 'why are you smiling more in the last six or seven years?' I say it's because I feel my colleagues are smiling too and that makes me feel really rewarded."

> 66
> Every Chinese
> New Year, for a
> week to 10 days,
> I visit around
> 100 hotels to
> say hello and
> celebrate the
> holidays with
> the staff. 99

IN HIS OWN WORDS

问答
Q&A

Q&A with Chief Executive David Sun

PERSPECTIVE ON A CHINESE COMPANY

What values drive Home Inns?

Our values emphasise happiness, love and helping people. Without love there is no passion for living. It is the basis of the business. If I'm not happy, how can I serve customers in a way that will make them happy? We senior managers should make people happy, but making people happy doesn't just mean giving them money.

We stress values like being respectful of people and being honest. When organisations get bigger and bigger, sometimes the only thing you can agree on is the basic thing about heart. Without this core shared value there can be a lot of conflict. There are 75,000 people in the organisation. You can have policies and procedures. But they depend on a foundation of core values.

What's your most urgent challenge?

The biggest challenge for a fast growing company is finding people with the right mindset and talent and finding enough of them. As you get bigger and more successful, there is a tendency for people in the organisation to believe that everything we do is right. The lack of new initiatives and entrepreneurial spirit is a potential threat. At our monthly management meetings I remind people that we are very young. We cannot rest on past accomplishments.

Are staffing needs changing?

As the business grows, the talents required for operating the business change. Today we have a multi-brand strategy with a high-end product and a low-end product. We need professionals who can run a more complicated business. Over the next eight-to-10 years, we plan to grow from 2,000 hotels and 75,000 people to possibly 5,000 hotels and 200,000 people. We may face a shortage of people interested in working in a service industry.

Doesn't a labour shortage in a country of over 1.3 billion people seem odd?

It does, but there are at least two reasons for it, both related to the improvement of China's economy. First, many of the workers came from the countryside. But life is improving in the countryside and there is less incentive for people to leave. Second, it's becoming more expensive to live in the cities. Although wages are rising, they may not be keeping pace with price increases. That disconnect slows the migration from the countryside to the cities.

CEO Sun with staff at Home Inns Shanghai headquarters.

" We stress values like being respectful of people and being honest. When organisations get bigger and bigger, sometimes the only thing you can agree on is the basic thing about heart. "

KEEPING PACE WITH RAPID CHANGE

How will you adjust to the labour problem?

Many people who go to cities for work plan to stay only for a short period to earn money before returning to the countryside and their family roots. Around 60 per cent of our hotels are in big cities. As we move to smaller cities we will try to staff hotels with local people. But the problem in smaller cities will be finding local people with suitable education.

That's why I think the government really wants more urbanisation. Urbanisation means not only that people move to the big cities, but also that industries move to the lower tier cities. That way, as China becomes wealthier, income, infrastructure, education, medical care and everything else is distributed more evenly throughout society.

How will businesses in China change over the next few years?

Companies need a breather. They need time to make improvements and refinements to help ensure that the next fast-growth period will be healthier. This is a national issue. We need to address problems of air and water pollution, for example. We don't believe that you can blame the past 30 years, because without that growth you don't have the increase in wealth.

Some people ask why the growth could not be achieved with better balance. Maintaining the right balance is difficult. We know this from running the company. During the past 10 years the top priority of our company was growth. We expanded at a pace of about one new hotel every day. Now we need to address the consequences of that growth with improvements in efficiency, profitability, human resources and systems.

Will there be any fundamental shifts beyond these improvements?

The biggest challenge in this country is the lack of a simple, unique value system. What I mean is that in the West you have a diversity of countries and peoples, but you share a common set of values, perhaps based in religion, that emphasise love and tolerance and the need to help people.

In China, we do not have this singular unifying value system. In the last 30 years, the emphasis has been on money and fortune. But now, more and more people don't believe this is right. Seeking money alone would be the wrong direction for Chinese society in the future. Money can never satisfy everybody. What's important is a shared belief in the value of each individual human being.

Maintenance worker in a Shanghai Home Inn.

> **❝**
> Companies
> need a breather.
> They need time to make
> improvements
> and refinements
> to help ensure
> that the next
> fast-growth
> period will be

CHINA AND THE WEST

What management challenges are particular to a Chinese company?

One of the hardest challenges is what Westerners say, "You never know what the Chinese people are thinking." Sometimes Chinese people don't know what their colleagues are thinking. So the biggest challenge is to create an environment where people feel that they can be open.

During the eight years I have been in this company, there are two activities I continued uninterrupted, even in 2008 when the budget was very tight. One is the annual party. The other is a three-day company event during the summer. We gather together about 2,000 people to dance and sing, play sports and just have fun.

Have you had success in encouraging openness?

When I first joined the company, I said hello to the person cleaning the office. She looked scared and walked away, probably thinking, "The big boss is coming." Today we have easy conversations and she feels comfortable even joking with me.

Before one of my colleagues retired several years ago, she came to my office and we had a long talk. Her prior experience was with an SOE (State Owned Enterprise) and she had a traditional Chinese management style. She said, "When you first arrived at the company, I doubted you would make these changes. But you did what you said you would do." The more you deliver on the commitment, the more things change.

> ❝ The Chinese market is so fast and so flexible, we don't stick so much to long-term strategy. Influenced by the Internet, the society is changing faster and faster, so the traditional Western way of long-term strategy is not really suitable. ❞

How else do western and Chinese businesses differ?

The Chinese market is so fast and so flexible, we don't stick so much to long-term strategy. Influenced by the Internet, the society is changing faster and faster, so the traditional Western way of long-term strategy is not really suitable.

Also, the Chinese companies and the western companies differ in their stages of development. The western companies are in a more mature stage. Their senior leaders are more likely to be professional managers. The Chinese companies are more often entrepreneurial. In a fast-changing business environment, the existing know-how of a professional manager sometimes isn't as useful as the entrepreneurial approach. Entrepreneurs may have less know-how, but they are constantly reevaluating the environment. The professional managers need know-how. Entrepreneurial managers need know-why.

Around 2,000 Home Inns staff members gather in Hangzhou for the annual three-day company outing designed to build teamwork and foster openness.

David Sun being tossed up in the air by Home Inn employees at Sports Day.

BUILDING A GLOBAL BRAND

Strengthening infrastructure, cultivating customer loyalty

" In the next eight-to-10 years, we want to reach 5,000 hotels. At that number, we will be among the top three hotel chains worldwide. But the goal over the next 10 years is not just about building scale but also the strength of the basic infrastructure of the company. We have more improvement to make when we benchmark ourselves against some of the world's leading hotel brands in terms of marketing, service, IT, staff training and other factors. It may take us more than 10 years to close the gap.

To become a global brand requires that we understand the relevant strengths of our company. Many Chinese companies expand abroad because they have the money for expansion. But it's about more than money. Money means that you have power to purchase, but it doesn't mean that you have power to operate. For us, the key factors of globalisation are strengthening the core competencies of our company and building up our customer base.

Currently, about 80 million Chinese people travel overseas annually. That number should almost double in the next 10 years. We need to build loyalty to the brand. That's critical for expansion globally. You need to go overseas with your customers. They carry the brand with them. Currently, most Chinese people travel abroad in tourist groups. As independent travel expands, our opportunity will increase. Once we are established in other markets we can expand in them. "

TODAY'S CUSTOMERS

Customers know, and expect, value

" The customers in China today are becoming more professional. They know the value of the product. Not many years ago, people stayed at a hotel because it was convenient, but they had no experience with standards of hospitality. Today, because they know more, in part because of the Internet, they expect more.

Before, customers did not share their candid opinion, especially if it was negative. So the feedback was unhelpful. Today, people are more direct. They will tell you, 'This is good or not good.'

I think that customer feedback originally was more of a western concept. The Internet facilitates openness about sharing information and opinions. The technology makes a big difference. For eastern people face-to-face commenting is much more difficult.

Actually, today we have too much feedback because so many people are on micro blogs. There is so much feedback it's not useful. As a business, we need to try and understand which comments are most useful for the customers and which the business can realistically respond to, based on our available resources, to make customers feel satisfied. "

上海华谊(集团)公司
SHANGHAI HUAYI (GROUP) COMPANY

CHEMICAL GIANT COMPETES AND COLLABORATES WITH MANY GLOBAL RIVALS

Shanghai Huayi (Group) Company

CHAIRMAN	LIU XUNFENG
INDUSTRY	CHEMICALS
OWNERSHIP	LOCAL SOE
SALES (2012)	RMB 444.4 BILLION ($72.5 BILLION)
HEADQUARTERS	SHANGHAI
YEAR FORMED	1996

Shanghai Huayi Group is one of China's largest manufacturers and marketers of chemical products. Through its more than 20 subsidiaries, the Group produces over 10,000 plastic and rubber products, such as tyres.

In 2008, Huayi streamlined a complicated corporate structure into five core businesses: energy, tyres, advanced materials, speciality chemicals and services.

The services business leverages Huayi's infrastructure to meet the cargo shipping and other needs of its western joint venture partners. This business fits with what the company calls its dual-core model, becoming a provider of both products and higher-margin services and consultation.

Similarly, the company developed a financial services division that provides financing for customers and partners. Along with enhancing profitability, the loan business is intended to strengthen customer relationships and long-term loyalty.

These developments are part of the company's strategy to both compete and collaborate with international companies. Huayi maintains 34 joint ventures with major global pharmaceutical, chemical and industrial brands such as DuPont, BASF, Bayer and Michelin.

Huayi employs almost 40,000 people in China. Established in 1996 from predecessor holding companies, the Shanghai Huayi Group traces its origins to the Shanghai Kalin Paint & Pigment Factory, China's first paint manufacturer, formed in 1915. Huayi remains committed to protecting Shanghai's environment and advancing the economic development of the city and the welfare of its inhabitants.

Vats and duct network at Huayi facility.

化工

Chemical
Manufacturing

BRAND STRENGTH

Unifying the brand
to maximise power

66

Brand is an important part of our core competitive power. I think that all Chinese businesses in the future will emphasise brand if they want to achieve sustained success.

Our brand management philosophy is that the Group does not compete with enterprises for profit and the enterprises do not compete with the Group for name. We use a double brand strategy.

The company name comes first, then the product brand. Huayi is our brand, but we also promote product brands. Our approach is analogous to how Passat is a product brand of VW and Buick is a product brand of GM.

We have been unifying our brand name. In pursuit of this strategy we abandoned an 87-year-old company brand, Dachunghwa Rubber Company, which was a difficult but necessary decision to achieve the idea of 'One Huayi'. 99

Chairman Liu Xunfeng

CHAIRMAN
LIU XUNFENG

Scientist CEO transforms business for global growth

Combines Chinese and western management styles

Liu Xunfeng is a scientist CEO and proactive manager.

Trained as a chemical engineer, Liu spent the early part of his career at Sinopec, China's oil and gas giant and one of the country's most strategically important State Owned Enterprises (SOE). He joined Sinopec in 1989 and rose to vice president of SPC, a Sinopec subsidiary, in nine years.

Liu gained experience running a large organisation when he managed a Sinopec plant in Shanghai. His global business perspective and English language skill come from a later assignment, heading a multi-billion dollar Sinopec joint venture with BP.

Subsequently, the Shanghai government appointed Liu vice president of Shanghai Chemical Industrial Park, south of the city, where BP, Bayer and other global petrochemical and pharmaceutical companies have research and development and production facilities.

Liu brought this blend of Chinese and western management experience to Huayi Group, when he arrived as president in 2007. Now chairman and CEO, he is one of

only 20 people awarded the title of Leader of Shanghai Industry and Business.

Still, even in the imposing corporate centre, located in the middle of Shanghai and surrounded by formal gardens, Liu can seem disarmingly personable and engaging.

When a photojournalist assigned to take a picture of Liu recommended rearranging furniture, Liu revealed his bias for action over hierarchy. Rather than contact staff, he began moving furniture himself, asking only, "Where do you want the chairs?"

> " We want Huayi to be thought of as China's leading chemical business. "

Chairman Liu outside Huayi corporate centre in downtown Shanghai.

Streamlining with western and Chinese approaches

When Liu arrived at Huayi he found an enormous business, with over 40,000 employees and a complex organisational structure that inhibited growth. Liu re-arranged more than a few chairs.

First, he streamlined the business to just five divisions, including consulting and financial services for generating higher margins and cultivating stronger client relationships. Second, he introduced a western-style matrix structure to manage the business.

In the matrix structure, each key executive becomes responsible for three areas: a vertical business, such as speciality chemicals; a horizontal function, like finance, across all the businesses; and a geographical region. The inclusion of regional responsibilities indicates Liu's belief in the importance of relationships.

"Relationships with the local government are critical," Liu said. "The sensitivity of the relationship and the need to display the appropriate level of respect, require that someone on a vice president level serve as our representative."

Leading by example, Liu included himself in the management matrix structure. Along with his key roles as Huayi Group chairman and CEO and party committee secretary, he also serves as the head of Double Coin, the Group's tyre business.

Implementation of the matrix structure requires leaders to effectively motivate staff.

Liu nurtures staff, sending promising executives to leading Chinese and international universities. Huayi maintains official relationships with Shanghai University of Finance and Economics and East China University of Science and Technology.

Facing pressures of both public and private company

Like Sinopec, Huayi Group is an SOE. The Chinese government owns a major stake, making the state both Liu's employer and his largest shareholder. Straddling state and public ownership, Huayi experiences the pressures of both worlds, but not all the potential benefits.

Huayi competes in a marketplace that includes other SOEs, international joint ventures and private entrepreneurial companies. It probably receives less state support than SOEs in which the government owns a larger stake. At the same time, Huayi must meet all the reporting requirements of a listed company, which limits its flexibility compared with private firms.

"We're in the middle," said Liu.

The need to simultaneously satisfy shareholders and comply with regulations while operating in a marketplace with a mix of publicly owned and private competitors would feel like familiar territory to CEOs of Western public companies. It's new to China.

Huayi operation at the Shanghai Chemical Industrial Park.

IN HIS OWN WORDS

Q&A with Chairman Liu Xunfeng

PERSPECTIVE ON A CHINESE COMPANY

How has Huayi changed under your leadership?

The business began its change in 2008. It's a good example of a transformed Shanghai SOE. Huayi had too many businesses, which hindered our competitive power. Now Huayi has five core businesses: energy, tyres, advanced materials, speciality chemicals and services.

The services business is part of what we call our "dual-core" business model. That means we operate both as a manufacturing business and also as a service provider. This strategy is similar to IBM's. We implemented the strategy in 2011. It enables us to leverage our knowledge and physical assets.

What would be an example of this business model?

We are a producer of chemical products. That means our capabilities include engineering, procurement and construction as well as logistics, packaging, sales and transportation. We provide bundles of these services to clients, such as BASF or Bayer, which outsource to us.

We also can offer financial services. China's regulatory commission recently licensed Huayi as a provider of financial services. In effect, we can help customers with their cash needs, for example. That builds loyalty.

What kind of company do you envision Huayi becoming?

We want Huayi to be thought of as China's leading chemical business. Currently, 80 per cent of our global revenue is in China. We see Huayi becoming a strong international player in the chemical business. It's a journey. Huayi began as a government bureau. We then became a business. We own a lot of land, but we have always emphasised that we are not a real estate company.

How will you drive growth?

The Chinese economy will continue to grow and the process of urbanisation will present many opportunities. Chinese businesses need to compete on an international level and seize opportunities overseas. Increase in volume is not the most important thing. The focus should be on improving the core competitive power of the business.

But it's not always about competition. Some of the growth will come from collaboration. Our relationships with DuPont, Michelin and BASF are such that we both compete and collaborate. We have 34 joint ventures. Joint ventures are another way to improve competitive power.

Double Coin tyres ready for fitting in a Shanghai garage.

> " Chinese businesses need to compete on an international level and seize opportunities overseas. Increase in volume is not the most important thing. The focus should be on improving the core competitive power of the business. "

KEEPING PACE WITH RAPID CHANGE

What's your key focus as chairman?

When you have the role of managing a company, you're responsible for controlling the overall direction of the company. Your main concern is thought leadership. There are changes on a day-to-day basis and these are important, of course. But I try to understand the large trends that will impact the business over time.

What trends do you look at?

Some influences are industry-specific. Consumers influence trends, but so do suppliers. The car manufacturers, as well as the rubber manufacturers, decide the industry trends for tyres, for example. You also need to consider what the competition is doing, or will do.

Other considerations are more global. Both the domestic and international economies have huge implications on the business. Other factors, such as the increased focus on the environment as well as on CSR (Corporate Social Responsibility) also concern me. The market is full of challenges. A business could fall behind at any moment. Therefore, a business has to be strong in human resources, capital, technology and management.

What is your personal management style?

I have a long-term vision and dreams. As CEO, I try to persuade the management team to arrive at this same outline. We have a culture of openness. We use different ways to communicate a sense of urgency.

We have held annual theory-discussion meetings since 2009. We have held annual CEO roundtable sessions since 2010. We also annually hold meetings with major clients, such as Baosteel and Sinopec. The business needs to transform. That can only happen through openness.

Is change the greatest challenge?

People often are afraid of change and think that the old way is best. It's not natural to want to change. But people have to see that the world is changing and we must change too. In fact, we try to project a sense of urgency that the world is changing and we will fail if we don't change with it.

CHINA AND THE WEST

How do you implement your western collaborative style?

It's important to say that it's not just about the leader having these thoughts, but also for the team to have the same idea. If the management team doesn't share this thought, then you can't implement anything.

Case studies are the best way to share this idea. I use successful case studies, such as the joint venture with BASF, to communicate that in the future we need to collaborate. Our numerous successful joint ventures with international companies demonstrate the necessity for collaboration. I have always spoken about the culture of Huayi, which is one of openness. Being open is even more important than reforming.

> 66
> I have many working partners and friends from foreign-capital investment enterprises and we exchange tips and experiences with each other. The key topics are about the Chinese and world economies and what the overseas companies are focussing on. 99

How do you manage such a complicated business?

We have 17 independent companies among our five core businesses. We implemented a matrix management structure in 2009. There are seven people in our management team. Each general manager is responsible for three roles.

A general manager heads one of the companies, but also oversees a particular function, like finance, across all the companies. And a vice president also oversees a particular geographic region across all the companies. The organisation is a matrix at most levels. It's critical to have clear boundaries. For example, the manager for Health, Safety and the Environment (HSE) for our Double Coin tyre business, reports both to the CEO of Double Coin and to the head of HSE for the Huayi Group.

Where did you get the inspiration for this management system?

It came from my experience in the joint venture with BP. This management style is what foreign-capital investment enterprises adopt. I have many working partners and friends from foreign-capital investment enterprises and we exchange tips and experiences with each other.

We hold an annual half-day CEO roundtable. We invite high-level management from foreign-investment enterprises, such as BASF, BP and DuPont. The key topics are about the Chinese and world economies and what the overseas companies are focussing on.

XIAMEN ITG GROUP

GROUP EXEMPLIFIES SUCCESS OF CHINA'S SPECIAL ECONOMIC ZONES

Xiamen ITG Group Corporation, Ltd.

贸易

Trading

CHAIRMAN	HE FULONG
INDUSTRY	CONGLOMERATE
OWNERSHIP	LOCAL SOE
SALES (2012)	RMB 46 BILLION ($7.5 BILLION)
HEADQUARTERS	XIAMEN
YEAR FORMED	1980

ITG Group is a large conglomerate with diversified interests managed through 16 subsidiaries. The key businesses include: trade and logistics, real estate development, optical electronics, culture and tourism and investment.

The trade business, for example, includes the import and export of natural resources as well as consumer products including cars and clothing. ITG also offers shipping, warehousing and other related logistical services. The company owns extensive real estate, with a concentration on upscale residential developments.

ITG Group was established in 1980, in Fujian Province on China's southeastern coast, in a Special Economic Zone. Listed on the Shanghai Stock Exchange in 1996, the company is publicly traded.

Some of the company's subsidiaries also are publicly traded. ITG Group is owned in part by the city of Xiamen.

Container ship in the port of Xiamen, where ITG has operations.

CHAIRMAN
HE FULONG

> 66 I have been here 12 years. That is a full cycle on the Chinese calendar. 99

Professional manager produces strong results

Seeks to balance growth with preservation of heritage

He Fulong heads one of China's largest diversified trading companies, based in Xiamen, among the country's first Special Economic Zones. As the chairman builds the company, he worries about balancing the pace of rapid growth with respect for China's past.

Trained as an accountant, Chairman He has overseen a period of consistent growth since joining ITG in 2001. Revenue has increased from around RMB 2.2 billion ($360 million) when He arrived, to RMB 46 billion ($7.5 billion) today. In 2006, He led the successful effort to list the ITG on the Shanghai Stock Exchange.

"I have been here 12 years. That is a full cycle on the Chinese calendar. Our management team is better informed and clearer about strategy. But we still need to unify our business more. That takes more time."

He believes that the company needs to find more sustainable businesses. The company had been one of China's largest suppliers of iron ore, for example, but factories have many sources for their raw materials, both in China and abroad.

"So we must develop a more vertical business that's not so dependent on natural resources. We need to continue to mine natural resources, but also invest in steel manufacturing. And we need to leverage our logistics and network advantages to expand the business and increase sales and profits."

ITG must simultaneously move forward and adjust as necessary along the way, He suggests, to balance speed with quality and the acceptance of western influence with the maintenance of Chinese distinctiveness.

He recalled a recent visit to Chengdu and being moved by the mountains and rivers of Sichuan and the preservation of Chinese heritage. "Here in Xiamen, the city is very modernised," he said. "But we have erased a lot of culture and Chinese heritage. Maybe we're moving too quickly. Slow is not necessarily better, but moving too fast can be like pulling on a plant to help it grow."

IN HIS OWN WORDS

Q&A with Chairman He Fulong

Q&A

PERSPECTIVE ON A CHINESE COMPANY

What business philosophy guides ITG?

The famous Chinese philosopher, Hu Shi, from the first half of the last century, said that you can dare to make big "ifs," but you must have small "proofs." We should be full of hopes and dreams, but in the practical world we must be steady and strong with our feet on solid ground. This philosophy guides ITG.

We seek steady improvement. Our goal is not size alone, but size that we achieve as a respected, exemplary organisation. Our name ITG means International Trading Group, but we take the letters to signify our core values. "I" is for integrity, being persistent in pursuit of our dreams. "T" is for trust, being faithful to our jobs and colleagues. "G" is for growth, which is the outcome.

What are the key contributors to the success of ITG?

As a preface, I'll first correct the impression that our business is so successful. We have enjoyed some success, but I believe that it's important to remain self-critical. We start with strategy. The strategy takes into account where we are now, our strengths and weaknesses, where we want to go and how we want to get there—what we will and will not do.

How do you form corporate strategy?

We rely on six Chinese characters to shape our strategic thinking. We organise these characters into three groups of two. The pairs of characters are: Respond and Make the Right Decision; Obtain and Drop; Study and Collaborate.

These pairs cause us to reflect. With every response we make, we need to consider whether it's right. When striving to obtain an objective, we need to drop our pursuit if the objective proves to be a bad choice or detrimental to the business. When we study, which is an important but solitary activity, we must be mindful of the need to collaborate, so that study is not simply academic, but leads to action and efficiency.

Can you summarise other parts of the business with Chinese characters?

Yes. Once you have a strategy, the next challenge is finding and cultivating the right people to help execute the strategy. All of us, myself included, are here to serve ITG. In a sense, people come first because people create the strategy. The Chinese word for enterprise or business is made up of several characters. The character symbolising "people" or "person" is on top and the character for "stop" is underneath, which implies that without people everything stops.

Shipping containers and hoists at the port in Xiamen.

> " We seek steady improvement. Our goal is not size alone, but size that we achieve as a respected, exemplary organisation. "

> 66
> We need to keep running fast, but also adjusting simultaneously to address important issues, such as quality and sustainability. 99

KEEPING PACE
WITH RAPID CHANGE

How has the business changed during the time that you've been with ITG??

This question is very difficult to answer. It's a long period of time. It's the full 12-year cycle of the Chinese zodiac. But I have been reflecting on this subject recently. I should say that our senior management team is much better informed today. Our strategy is much clearer.

We're more confident about our direction. At the same time, it's important to remember that the company is just 32 years old. We are not like a business that has been established for 100 years. There are levels of greater coordination and sharpening core competencies that grow better with more time. We have more improvements to make..

What will be your top priority over the next few years?

I think we still want to go back to the original thought of "cash is king." This is what we must remember in the next few years. You could have a lot of ambition and everything lined up, but you won't be able to do anything without cash. That's why it's the most important thing. Perhaps I think that way because I used to be an accountant. To do your job well as CEO, you must control the cash well. This is our first commandment.

What will be your second priority?

The second thing I often say is, "adjust as you run." In the past, we sometimes ran too quickly, with little regard for the staff and team left behind and this is something we have to avoid. We need to keep running fast, but also adjusting simultaneously to address important issues, such as quality and sustainability.

CHINA AND THE WEST

How will China's economy perform in the near future?

I'm not an economist and cannot offer an expert opinion. But I can share my experience. Recently, I had dinner with a group of 18 senior managers and I posed this multiple-choice question to all of them: What do you think our business will be like next year—better, worse or not sure? Half of the group answered, better. And half answered, unsure. No one said that business would be worse.

This response in part reflects their Chinese ways. For example, if I invite a western person to my home and ask if the guest would prefer coffee or tea, I get a definitive response. A Chinese visitor is more likely to answer, "Whatever you prefer." I realise that some who responded positively to my poll may have held a negative opinion. Still, research I've seen and other factors make me tentatively optimistic about the economy.

What other factors influence your optimism?

First, there has been research that shows that the economy improves the year following a change in the government and party. Second, urbanisation is still going strong. The needs of people in the cities drive growth. Third, the government is paying more and more attention to improving people's lives and driving consumption.

How do you see the place of China in the global economy?

It's over 30 years since our economy opened at the end of the 1970s. We immediately became the world's workshop, producing low cost goods for the West, which brought wealth into the country. We were a poor country working for rich countries that created financial products to sell back to us. This cycle has changed.

The workshop has moved to other countries, like Vietnam and Malaysia. But those counties are too small to provide enough resources to support the old pattern, so it can't last long. And it's important to note that the global economy is about more than economics. It depends on many factors including: politics, history, geography, military power and currency fluctuations. It's very hard to have a clear vision. In all, China has a bright future, but the plan must be prudent.

Do people in the West understand China?

I believe that people misunderstand China. Usually, they have an opinion on one extreme or the other. Some people take a political position and demonise China. Others take a more cultural view and mythologise China. Both of these perspectives are limited and distorted. China is neither as terrible and chaotic as some people allege, nor is it as great as other people assert. The reality is in the middle. China is moving forward continuously.

MANAGING PEOPLE

Drawing wisdom from China's past

66 Managing a large workforce is critical but challenging. To explain the ITG approach I need to provide some background. It comes from a writer named Sima Guang, who lived in the 11th century during the Song Dynasty.

He wrote about the ideas of Cao Cao, a famous king, military leader and strategic thinker during the Three Kingdoms Period. Cao Cao believed that any person—even someone petty or corrupt—could be talented and make an important contribution.

Sima Guang disagreed. He organised humanity along two dimensions: knowledge and ethics. He then divided people into four groups. People at the extremes are: the 'saintly,' those endowed with both knowledge and ethics; and the 'foolish,' those lacking both knowledge and ethics. In the middle are: the 'good,' lacking knowledge but having ethics; and the 'petty,' having knowledge but lacking ethics.

Sima Guang argued that 'petty' people should never be used in an enterprise, but people from the other three classifications would be fine. I disagree with Cao Cao and with Sima Guang. Both views are oversimplified. The institution can control 'petty' people. And there are not many 'saintly' people in the world.

Most people are a mix, sometimes 'petty' and sometimes 'good.' A person who seems like a saint is probably faking it. In a business organisation, a good management system helps build individual loyalty and unify people around common goals.

This unity can be achieved when people exhibit three qualities: being honest, being reasonable and being willing to work hard and earn their salary. The core of accounting is to establish comprehensive management systems with a clear organisational structure that enables people to understand their responsibilities and roles.

You need to watch out for people who say they're motivated by 'love of party' or 'love of country.' They're being false. 99

Towers at the port in Xiamen.

UNDERSTANDING CHINA

Preconceptions usually wrong

" I am 60 years old this year. As children we read histories about Great Britain and we read the books of Charles Dickens. After visiting Britain a few times your preconception changes. Not to say that we understand Britain, but at least we no longer either demonise or mythologise the country. Similarly, people should come to China more often to have a look around. In the past 30 or 40 years the country has changed. It's opened up since I was a boy. There is a Chinese saying, 'Seeing once is better than hearing 100 times.' "

NCAM 新华资产

ASSET MANAGEMENT COMPANY POWERED BY CHINA INSURANCE INDUSTRY GROWTH

New China Asset Management Company, Ltd.

金融
Finance

ASSISTANT PRESIDENT	**ALICE FAN YANG**
INDUSTRY	ASSET MANAGEMENT FOR INSURANCE COMPANIES
OWNERSHIP	LOCAL SOE
SALES (2012)	RMB 430 BILLION ($70.3 BILLION)
HEADQUARTERS	BEIJING
YEAR FORMED	2006

Primarily engaged in assent management for New China Life Insurance Company, one of the country's leading insurers, NCAM also manages capital for other organisations and provides investment consultancy services.

Since its establishment in 2006, as one of China's earliest insurance asset management companies, total assets under management have grown at an annual rate exceeding 20 per cent.

The company employs 130 people and operates from a central office in Beijing, with plans for a Hong Kong office opening during the fall of 2013.

Listed on the Hong Kong and Shanghai Stock Exchanges, NCAM is 97 per cent owned by New China Life Insurance Company Ltd., whose main products include personal and group life insurance along with wealth management services. The controlling shareholder is Central Huijin Investment, Ltd.

Specialists developing financial analysis.

ASSISTANT PRESIDENT
ALICE FAN YANG

Executive gains education, career success in the West

But returns to China for greater opportunity

The name Alice Fan Yang says a lot.

It expresses the identity of the assistant president of NCAM, a Chinese born and educated adult with experience working and studying in the West. But the name does not reveal the changing dynamics of that identity.

As the assistant president of New China Asset Management, Yang is responsible for RMB 430 billion ($70.3 billion) of investment capital held by New China Life Insurance, one of China's top three life insurance companies.

She deeply understands both Chinese and Western ways of business. After earning a degree in economics from People's University in Beijing and an MBA from the University of Southern California in Los Angeles, Yang worked in investment banking and financial consulting in the US and Hong Kong.

Despite their successes overseas, Yang and her husband decided to return to China for both personal and business reasons. They missed their home country. And China today offers much greater advancement opportunities than when they left to pursue careers abroad.

In part because of these opportunities, they wanted their young daughter to finish her education in China. Doing business is more complicated in China than in the West, Yang believes. And China is changing rapidly. If their daughter were educated abroad, she'd have difficulty catching up.

"When I returned to Beijing after spending many years abroad, it was difficult for me just to cross the street. In the West the traffic is well regulated. In China it seems chaotic. You cannot just wait. You need to understand the traffic, make a choice and cross. It's a metaphor for life and business and understanding takes time."

NEW CHINA ASSET MANAGEMENT COMPANY, LTD.

Despite their successes overseas, Yang and her husband decided to return to China for both personal and business reasons. They missed their home country.

IN HER OWN WORDS

问答

Q&A

Q&A with Assistant President Alice Fan Yang

PERSPECTIVE ON A CHINESE COMPANY

What key challenges confront the insurance business?

The life insurance industry remains highly regulated. As a result, most life insurance products are still similar, so competitive differentiation is difficult. Companies need to become more creative. Now there's a potential threat of online insurance sales, which significantly lowers marketing costs. It would be difficult to compete with a company selling simple, easily understood insurance products online.

Do Chinese and western attitudes about insurance differ?

Chinese people like to spend money to make more money. They don't want to just spend money on insurance. They want a return, a dividend coming back on their investment. In the West it's normal to spend money on medical or car insurance. It's not that way in China. Chinese people see insurance as an expense.

Given this mentality, how will China's insurance industry thrive in the future?

Wealthier people tend to spend money on insurance. Plus, we will need to create products that offer both risk coverage and investment return. Along with creating the right products, we will need to have a sales force that can sell these kinds of products. Many of the sales people are poorly educated individuals who recently moved from the countryside to the city in search of opportunity. It requires selecting people who have reached a certain level of schooling and then educating them about insurance.

How do you manage that risk?

There's a Chinese saying: "Clear water has no fish." In other words, impurity is a by-product of simply being alive. In the context of business, it's normal that some mistakes will happen during the course of rapid growth. Similarly, the way we cross the street, with traffic moving in all directions and drivers ignoring the lights, is a good metaphor for operating in China. The rules are not as apparent as in the West. People sense how to navigate the apparent chaos and decide when to cross. Otherwise, you could wait all day.

Reception at Beijing headquarters.

COMMUNICATION

Listening for the meaning unsaid between the lines

66

When you do business in Chinese society, you need to have a feeling for what's unsaid between the lines. Having spent time in the West, when I communicate with western people, I speak directly. But in China, you need to hear what's behind the lines.

That's difficult for western people to understand. They think, 'You're wasting my time.' But listening closely is time well spent. This sensitivity is important especially when dealing with government officials. You will need to deal with the government and it's important to know what a government official is saying and why. 99

KEEPING PACE WITH RAPID CHANGE

What changes in China have most affected your industry?

We've seen dramatic changes in just the past two or three years. In the past, regulations limited the activities of insurance company investment banks and retail banks to their speciality. Insurance companies could only offer insurance, for example.

Now it's possible to become a financial services company and offer a full range of products. Everything is open. That means as a businessperson you need to have much more knowledge beyond your narrow speciality. You need to know every product. You need to understand the risks.

How do you manage with such a major development?

It's a strain. But it's like everything in China. It's moving so fast, you need to keep up. Sometimes it can be very frustrating. You don't feel like everything is under control. But you have to move.

Sometimes it's just the environment pushing you. Even if you don't want to move, you feel consumers pushing you: "Your competitor has this product. Why don't you?" So you move because you don't want to be left behind. Chinese people are aggressive about wanting new kinds of products.

What do you think drives this kind of aggressiveness?

In the past, we didn't have the freedom to choose a good life. Before the reforms, everyone had the same living standard. Everyone made the same money. No one needed to lock the door because everyone was poor and no one had special possessions.

Today people have more economic freedom. People are getting rich. They can have a car, travel overseas or get a better education. And they have access to more knowledge. You see people who are proud of creating new things. People seem satisfied.

NEW CHINA ASSET MANAGEMENT COMPANY, LTD.

CHINA AND THE WEST

What advice do you have for Westerners unaccustomed to the speed in China?

Be more observant. Take time to really understand what you're seeing. In China, even if the light is green, it's not necessarily your signal to safely cross. You need to make some judgments. And those judgments are based on experience. If you expect western rules, you may not like what you see.

Sometimes there's pushing, no lining up, no queuing. It's a developing country and it's not always polite. But there are reasons why some Chinese people are not following the rules. Some people have a lot of money and they show off. On the other side, people who recently arrived in the cities from the countryside may be struggling with poverty.

How is doing business in China different?

Doing business in the West is much easier than doing business in China. In general, business in the West is governed by rules. When rules are broken there are many channels for complaint, such the courts or the media.

China is changing. There are more regulations. But it's not the same as in the West. You are more on your own without a guide. And you need to find your way out. So the business environment is more complicated.

NCAM carefully selects staff and provides extensive education about the insurance industry.

What do you say to those who advise China to simply copy the West?

Chinese business people are learning from the West. They think that western business is their model. I think that we can learn from the West, but the West doesn't need to tell us what to do. I go to management companies overseas to learn. We're studying hard and we're learning. We're learning quickly.

For example, I spent time last year with Goldman Sachs because I know they have a better investment management system in terms of how to evaluate risk; how to make investment decisions; how to select your team; how to manage your team and how to generate investment return for your shareholders.

What can the West learn from China?

It will be difficult for a western businessperson to succeed in China without taking the time to understand. This is how I learn. When I'm in the West, the knowledge I gain is not only from my MBA courses. When I travel in the United States, for example, I try to understand the people and their mentality. In the United States I try to understand how people of so many different backgrounds work together in harmony.

Western business people need to learn more about the Chinese culture and society. They need to learn more about how Chinese business people think. Business thinking is rooted deeply in Chinese culture. Western business people need an appreciation of this culture to gain insight into how Chinese business people think and why they act as they do.

R&D WITH GLOBAL PARTNERS EMPOWERS ELECTRONICS SPECIALIST

Shenzhen Refond Optoelectronics Company, Ltd.

科技
Technology

CEO	GONG WEIBIN
INDUSTRY	LED TECHNOLOGY
OWNERSHIP	LISTED COMPANY
SALES (2012)	RMB 500 MILLION ($82.1 MILLION)
HEADQUARTERS	SHENZHEN
YEAR FORMED	2000

Refond specialises in energy-saving LED technology for a variety of applications, including indoor and outdoor lighting, digital screen backlighting and automotive instrument panels.

The company divides its business into five specialities: television, mobile devices, automotive, illumination and infrared. It operates several factories in China. The largest opened in Shenzhen during 2012.

Refond collaborates on laboratory work with the Konka Group, the Chinese consumer electronics company. Corporate partners also include Avago Technologies and 3M.

To drive innovation, Refond maintains research and development strategic alliances with Tsinghua University and Shenzhen University. Refond applied for 136 patents during 2012.

The company operates an extensive network of more than 30 sales offices throughout China and works with agents in the United States, Germany, Israel, Italy, Japan, South Korea, Russia, Turkey, the United Kingdom and the United States.

To increase financial strength, in an industry filled with competitors from the mainland and Taiwan, Refond filed an IPO in July 2011 and is listed on the Shenzhen Stock Exchange.

CONTEXT INSIGHT

★

Consumer Electronics

Shoppers desire both the Chinese and foreign brands

The world's largest consumer electronics market, China is expected to produce over $150 billion in electronic retail sales by 2015, presenting both foreign and Chinese brands with great potential.

The brands Chinese consumers select depend on what they're buying. Foreign brands typically dominate the market for TVs, other home entertainment devices and mobile phones. But even in flat-panel TVs, Chinese brands, such as Hisense, Changhong and Skyworth have made considerable progress entering the consideration set of Chinese consumers.

Chinese brands are especially strong in home appliances or "white goods." The market leaders, Haier and Midea, enjoy strong bonding with consumers, especially in Tier 1 cities, according to a 2011 study based on WPP's BrandZ™ brand analytic and equity database.

Haier scores favourably in Value-D, a BrandZ™ metric that indicates how well brands have balanced price and desirability. Consumers view Haier as a good value, offering quality at a fair price. Haier also scores well on TrustR, the BrandZ™ measurement of how much consumers trust a brand and are likely to recommend it. In the 2013 BrandZ™ Top 50 Most Valuable Chinese Brands, Haier ranked 30 and Midea 34. Gree, another leading Chinese appliance brand, ranked 28.

Research and analysis by Millward Brown, a WPP company

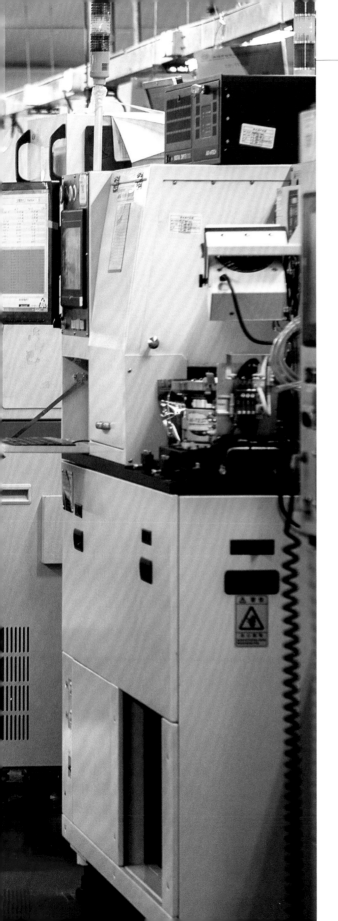

Inside an electronics workroom.

CEO
GONG WEIBIN

Company founder still building and learning

Quest for excellence tops money motive

> My original motivation was only to make money. But over time, building an excellent company became more important and making money became less important.

Gong Weibin established Refond in 2000.

He'd entered the electronics industry as a marketer, in 1994, developing the mainland business for a Taiwanese company. The company appointed Gong to cultivate lower income customers, until then a relatively ignored segment of the market. With that initiative, Refond Optoelectronics was formed.

Born and raised in the coastal province of Zhejiang, Gong Weibin left as a young man in search of greater opportunity in Shenzhen, which at the time was more open for commercial enterprise than Zhejiang.

Gong arrived in Shenzhen without a plan, but with self-confidence, imbued by his parents, that he would achieve success. His father is an educator, the head of a primary school. Gong had been a good student. His friends also valued education.

"I worked hard in school because I didn't want to disappoint my parents," said Gong, who returns to visit his parents roughly every other month.

Gong chose the electronics industry from many opportunities in China's burgeoning economy. Today, as the CEO, he spends time on strategy and helping staff members develop and assume greater responsibility.

"My original motivation was only to make money," Gong said. "But over time, building an excellent company became more important and making money became less important."

For Gong, excellence means more than being successful in a particular business. It means leveraging knowledge and expertise to innovate in related businesses. Always looking for new ideas, Gong tries to read a book a week, including history, philosophy, fiction or business. Even playing golf becomes a learning experience.

"Golf gets me in contact with many different kinds of people," said Gong. "We learn from each other."

SHENZHEN REFOND OPTOELECTRONICS COMPANY, LTD.

IN HIS OWN WORDS

问答

Q&A

Q&A with CEO Gong Weibin

PERSPECTIVE ON A CHINESE COMPANY

What is your vision for the future of the company?

I will personally be spending much time and effort making Refond a more exceptional company, especially on the management level. We will be inviting a lot of our staff to help make this vision happen. When the core members of our team are doing well, it will mean that I have done a good job and the company is a successful one. My vision is for more of our staff to become successful at management and operations.

Where do you look for inspiration and strength?

All people want to better themselves and become more exceptional. I often think and study about these topics: What is the core value of being alive and living in our society? For what purpose are we alive in our world? Now that I have money and the business is doing well and if I am granted more years of life, what kind of things could I do and create to leave behind? What can I leave behind for society, for my family?

Are there certain companies or brands that exemplify excellence for you?

I really admire Philips. It's a partner company. We make a lot of things for them. From working with Philips, you get the feeling that they don't have an "owner," not in a real sense. Even though they were not working for a specific boss and no one was forcing them, the staff sometimes would work until one or two in the morning to meet a deadline.

When people are up for doing this, it reflects the excellence of a company. Some Chinese companies simply do not have the infrastructure set up in a way to give ordinary people the space to do extraordinary things. At Philips, the infrastructure is set up for this. This is what I hope for Refond. We want people to flourish in our company and if everyone worked in this way the company would be one of the best.

Technicians work in a purified environment.

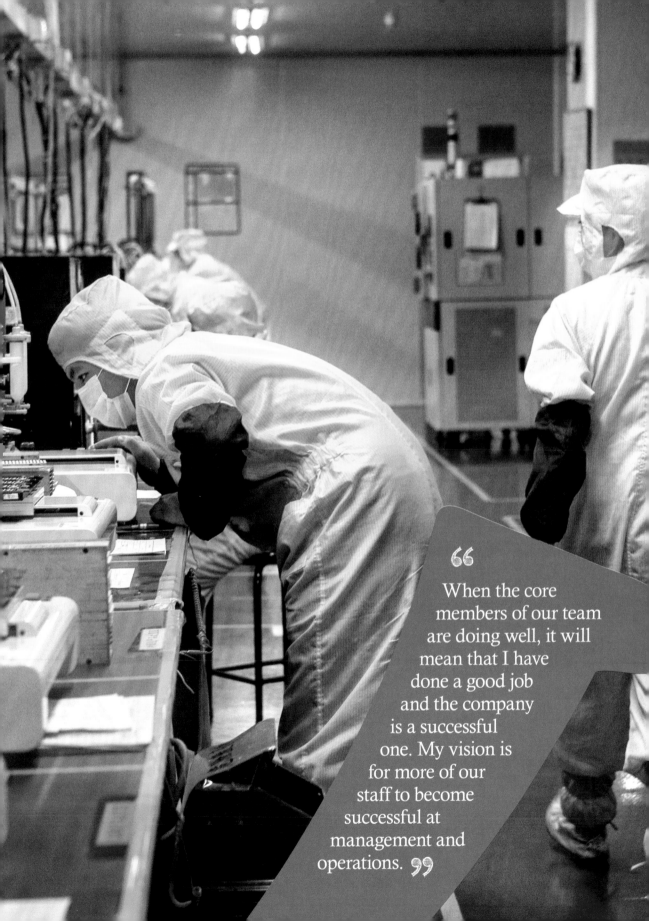

> 66
> When the core
> members of our team
> are doing well, it will
> mean that I have
> done a good job
> and the company
> is a successful
> one. My vision is
> for more of our
> staff to become
> successful at
> management and
> operations. 99

KEEPING PACE WITH RAPID CHANGE

What do you think your staff find positive about working at Refond?

They like that Refond strives to be a better company. Also, we are a very open company, certainly when compared with some private companies or family businesses. For example, none of my relatives work in the company and it's the same for our vice presidents and other managers. In some companies there is much more nepotism. We are not like this. And even though our company is quite small, our goal is to become a big company.

Growth requires management. How do you keep your knowledge fresh?

We gain specialised knowledge through communication with other companies and other specialists. Because of my responsibilities, it is not possible to go very deeply into some of these topics. I leave that to the specialists. But I closely follow the development of the industry.

For high-level management thinking we participate in MBA classes and receive systematic education about business management. And we encourage self-education. I have a personal target of reading at least 50 books every year. I have to read one book a week. My office shelves are filled with books.

What are your favourite management books?

I like *Built to Last* by Jim Collins and Jerry I. Porras. Another is *Amoeba Management* by Kazuo Inamori. These books have had a big impact on me. They were quite related to what I was thinking about anyway. *Built to Last* talks about how it is not only opportunity that makes a successful business. *Amoeba Management* talks about the development of the staff being more important than the needs of the shareholders. But, in general, belief and philosophy, things from my heart rather than management theory, have more of an influence on me.

Handling sensitive electronics.

CONTEXT INSIGHT

Golden Weeks

Electronic sales spike during special holidays

Sales for both foreign and domestic home electronic brands spike dramatically during the Golden Weeks, holiday periods created to drive consumption. Three-quarters of consumers in Tier 2 and 3 cities say that the Golden Weeks—Labour Day in the spring and National Day in the fall—are the best times of year for shopping and promotions on appliances and consumer electronics.

In Tier 2 and 3 cities, 44 per cent of consumers named National Day as the most important holiday for electronics shopping. Consumer priorities differ by city tier. In Tier 1 cities consumers regard status and style as important, while in the lower tiers consumers are more concerned with practical factors like reliability. Media spending across categories peaks during Golden Weeks.

PER CENT OF CONSUMERS

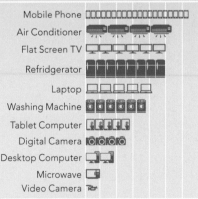

0 5 10 15 20 25 30 35

- Mobile Phone
- Air Conditioner
- Flat Screen TV
- Refridgerator
- Laptop
- Washing Machine
- Tablet Computer
- Digital Camera
- Desktop Computer
- Microwave
- Video Camera

Sales of appliances and home electronics spike throughout China during the Golden Weeks. Mobile phones, air conditioners, TVs and refrigerators are the most sought after electronic purchases during Labour Day in Tier 2 and 3 cities.

Source: Millward Brown 2012 Golden Weeks Shopper Behaviour Study

CHINA AND THE WEST

Do you think Chinese brands can become global?

This is tricky. The final output of a company is not its products, but its brand and its values. The world disapproves of China. The West sees China as a communist country, so it's biased against things that come from China, whether Refond or Haier. China's big brands are big because of support from the government, so these kinds of brands can't really win respect globally.

What steps can Chinese brands take if they aspire to become global?

If you want people to truly like you, then it's not only about having a good product, but having good values. The rapid growth of the past several decades has had an impact on values. This really is a problem. It doesn't come from the enterprises, but is a product of the environment of China currently. Most Chinese brands are not really at the level of being respected or considered inspirational.

Do you think Refond could be a global brand?

I think it would be hard for us because we are B2B and I think ultimately brand building is something more crucial for B2Cs. It would be hard for us, but this shouldn't hold us back from being a good company. I think it would be hard for us to become a strong brand, but we can be a strong company.

What challenges do you face internationally?

The overseas market is one of the biggest problems companies like ours face. We are not international enough yet. We lack talent that meets international standards and we have few solutions for this shortcoming. One solution is to recruit talent from overseas. Another option is to improve through mergers and acquisitions or joint ventures with foreign companies that are similar to us. Also, we have a lot of communication and cultural exchange with major overseas companies, especially through the illumination part of the business.

What can Chinese companies learn from the West?

We work mainly with large foreign companies. My impression is that they work in a systematic way. I think Chinese companies could learn from this example. A lot of Chinese companies rely on the "boss." At some of the largest Chinese companies, major decisions are made by only one or two people. Foreign companies rely more on teams.

What can western companies learn from China?

The strengths of Chinese companies come from something that is inherent in the Chinese people. Having suffered so long in poverty, the Chinese are very industrious. I think in the West people don't want work as hard. They work only to the level of OK. At Chinese companies, people are happy to work overtime until 10 pm for no extra pay.

Western companies could learn that there are people who just want to make the company the best. I think we are not as good from the management side, but we have this deep longing in our hearts, which is a strength that the West lacks.

Specialised equipment is constantly monitored.

66
Western
companies could learn
that there are people who just
want to make the company the best.
I think we are not as good from the
management side, but we have this
deep longing in our hearts, which is
a strength that the West lacks. 99

Safewell

SECURITY PRODUCT BRAND BENEFITS FROM CHINA'S GROWING AFFLUENCE

Safewell Group Holdings, Ltd.

CHAIRMAN	XU PUNAN
INDUSTRY	SECURITY EQUIPMENT AND DEVICES
OWNERSHIP	PRIVATE
SALES (2012)	RMB 8 BILLION ($1.3 BILLION)
HEADQUARTERS	NINGBO, ZHEJIANG
YEAR FORMED	1998

Safewell Group Holdings Ltd. operates as a conglomerate of 10 subsidiaries that are engaged primarily in the design, manufacture and marketing of electronic security and precision sheet metal products.

The product range includes safes for various applications along with electronic and building access security devices, digital locks and secure metal cabinets for computer equipment.

Safewell invests heavily in innovation, research and development and state-of-the-art production technology. It also strives to constantly improve its worldwide delivery speed and after-sales service.

Founded in 1998 as a family business based in southeastern China, in Zhejiang Province, Safewell now employs around 5,000 people and operates globally, with a presence in Hong Kong, Southeast Asia, the Middle East, Japan, the US, Canada, Germany, France, Turkey and South Africa. Safewell originated as an OEM (Original Equipment Manufacturer) and ODM (Original Design Manufacturer).

Safewell safes, for various functions, in a Shanghai shop.

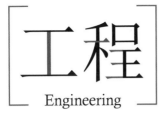

Engineering

CONTEXT INSIGHT

★

Consumer Trust

Safety problems erode consumer trust in brands

Product safety is an urgent concern for Chinese consumers. Recent scandals, about tainted milk or faulty automobile parts, not only affected particular industries but also eroded consumer trust over all.

Trust scores of the BrandZ™ Top 50 Most Valuable Chinese Brands and of China's 30 most trusted brands, have decreased steadily since 2011. In this world of declining trust, trust becomes a strategic imperative for brand success. BrandZ™ is WPP's brand analytics and equity database.

The rapid erosion of trust is due in part to pervasive social media and the immediate and widespread publicity that surrounds brand shortcomings. China leads the world in mobile phones and has 591 million Internet users, according to the China Internet Network Information Center.

Strengthening trust and recommendation is essential for brand success in China. While a brand associated with safety, like Safewell, has an advantage, brands generally can improve levels of trust and recommendation by consistently adhering to certain strategies and practices, including:

- Transparency: Immediate acknowledgment, apology and remediation help minimise loss of trust.

- Connection: Emotional connection with consumers through high levels of service and personal interaction can help minimise loss of trust.

- Alliances: Relationships with brands known for strict production and safety standards demonstrate a genuine desire to gain knowledge and improve.

One insight relates to the reawakening interest in Chinese culture and customs as a counterpoint to the frenzy of modern life. According to BrandZ™ analysis, consumers assess the character of the most trusted Chinese brands as wise, friendly and caring, characteristics that are deeply rooted in Chinese traditions.

Research and analysis by Millward Brown, a WPP company

CHAIRMAN
XU PUNAN

Buddhist view shapes entrepreneur's values

Strives to generate profit and happiness

Two Chinese words—da ai—best summarise Chairman Xu Punan's business philosophy. They mean literally "big love."

The term implies a deep sense of humanity matched with optimism and awe for life. It's a Buddhist world view from which Xu derives the values that shape his business. For Xu, manufacturing and marketing security products advances his larger goal: to bring more happiness into the world by improving the security and contentment people experience in their lives.

Xu matches these values with commercial instincts gained growing up around Ningbo, in Zhejiang Province, along China's southeastern coast near Shanghai. The inhabitants of this densely populated region, historically subject to foreign influence, are considered to be open to new ideas and innovation. And the region is known for producing entrepreneurs, sometimes referred to as the Ningbo clan.

Xu personifies this combination of religious values and business acumen and drive. He's affable, wears a fashionable trilby hat and a quality watch. He recently purchased a vineyard in France that supplies wine for the cellar in the villa Xu built next to the factory in China.

"I hope members of my staff are happy," he says. "Because only with happy staff can we consistently deliver high quality products."

Xu came from a modest background. In a traditional Chinese way, his family felt it was its duty to help launch Xu in a career. Xu first attended school to become an electrical engineer. After graduation, he joined his older brother in business.

The decision to manufacture and market safes was well considered and strategic. Chinese people, in general, are great savers. As affluence increases, they're saving more. The Chinese also are sceptical of large institutions like banks. With this combination of factors—a society of savers with a need for a place to keep their greater wealth—the safe business seemed like a safe bet.

The brothers eventually split the business with Xu taking responsibility for international and his brother focussed on domestic. Safewell now markets worldwide and is opening overseas production facilities. But Xu rejects acquisition candidates that match Safewell's business if they don't share its values.

"Our work can be both tiring and enjoyable. What's really exhausting is not when the body is tired, but when the heart and mind are tired. It's not sustainable if we only strive for a profit without helping people."

SAFEWELL GROUP HOLDINGS, LTD.

> **"** I hope my staff members are happy. Because only with happy staff can we consistently deliver high quality products. **"**

IN HIS OWN WORDS

Q&A

Q&A with Chairman Xu Punan

PERSPECTIVE ON A CHINESE COMPANY

> 66
> Delivering product quality and customer care are our most important goals. To accomplish them we must do everything well. We must tighten every screw well and look after even the tiniest detail. 99

What are the brand values that you believe are important?

Safewell is a family business. We started by manufacturing safes. That means our core customers are fairly wealthy. But our business also is about fulfilling my personal aspiration: To help others. This makes me happy.

Delivering product quality and customer care are our most important goals. To accomplish them we must do everything well. We must tighten every screw well and look after even the tiniest detail. This is the only way to make a high quality product and only then will the client be satisfied. We must constantly realise the promise that our name implies. Everything must be safe and well.

What influenced you most in forming these values?

I derive these values from the Buddha and the books of Buddhism. Reading the books of Buddhism is a way for me to understand the meaning of life. I work to communicate the central value of my business. What I am trying to communicate and deliver is "big love." By that I mean I wish to help more people.

In my business I hope to nurture more entrepreneurs who have the same values as I, to spread this "big love." If I nurture one hundred entrepreneurs and each of them nurtures another hundred, this cultural heritage of "big love" will be passed down and improve society and the lives of the people.

Safes inside and out.

Are these values similar to CSR (Corporate Social Responsibility)?

There are many levels of CSR. It's not possible unless the company is successful. The first priority is to have everyone in the company understand that the customer is like the sky, everywhere and of the highest importance. Making a profit depends on satisfying the customer. Then, when we are making profit, the staff must be respected and rewarded. Their livelihoods need to be guaranteed and their incomes need to be improved.

Taking good care of staff is a fundamental part of CSR. We do this part. We do it without seeking publicity. It's something you do, not something you talk about. Maybe there will be a business return. It's about having an outcome that follows from doing the right thing.

BRAND NAME

The Feng Shui of Safewell

Feng Shui is the ancient Chinese custom of finding the right balance of energy flow to maximise personal wellbeing. It is important when choosing a name.

The Safewell name in Chinese is Shengwei, 盛威. Sheng means strong. Wei means prestige or influence. In combining the two words into a name the company founders signified that strength is required to start a company and prestige assures its sustained existence. Xu and his brother had in mind inner strength and prestige attained from performing honestly a and promising only what the company can deliver.

The founders also wanted a name that suggested modest aspirations, so they avoided any words that implied great height or size. The fact that the word sheng is similar in sound to shen, the Chinese for kidneys, adds an additional layer of meaning however, because in Chinese medicine the kidneys are considered a foundation to good health.

In translating the name to English as Safewell, Chairman Xu tried to reflect the perspective of customers who aspire to be happy—financially secure and worry free. The name of the company also communicates a message to its employees: We want you to be happy too; only happy staff can consistently deliver high quality products.

KEEPING PACE WITH RAPID CHANGE

How do you find people to work at Safewell who share the company's values?

It's not easy. But people are the most important element in the business. There is very good return for investment in the right people. When I find someone who shares the company's values, someone in whom I see potential, I disregard their current state. I don't care if they're far along in their career and having a hard time, or if they're just out of school and have little experience. I will try my best to train and develop them.

Once you have the right people, how do you motivate them?

People are driven and guided by ideas. A person might give his or her life for an idea, but a person rarely would die for a physical thing. It's important to inspire people to reach the level of ideas. They can specialise in a job for which they have competence and which gives them pleasure. We have our own business school and middle to high-level managers all have been through there to train and study. The challenge is to have all the people subscribe to the same core values regardless of their job. We coach people to work to make life better.

Do you have particular motivational tactics?

There isn't only one way. And it also depends on the experience of the staff. We were reminded of this lesson not long ago. To motivate our staff we present valuable annual awards, such as cars and houses, to the highest performers. It is a good programme, but a recent result was funny and unexpected. When one of our employees received a car, he said he appreciated the recognition, but what he really needed was a girlfriend. We try to give people what they need. It's not always possible.

Does everyone in the organisation receive coaching?

The things spoken about at each level are different. We may communicate an idea one way to the management leaders and another way to staff. If we don't communicate clearly then it's wasted breath. But it is not the fault of the person to whom we are speaking. It is our fault for not communicating effectively. We believe in addressing people with respect.

Retail display of Safewell products.

> 66
> We have our
> own business school
> and middle to high-level
> managers all have
> been through
> there to train
> and study.
> The challenge
> is to have all
> the people
> subscribe
> to the same
> core values
> regardless of

CHINA AND THE WEST

What is the key to succeeding internationally?

International business is important to our company. I think of international business in the way our solar system works. All the planets have their own orbit around the sun. But all the planets are subject to the same forces. Similarly, companies have their own interests but they can do business with each other when they share values.

For example, besides China, I'm interested in the United States. It contains many cultures and the spirit of freedom to accept ideas from elsewhere. It is a large market and we can gain a worthwhile share of the market. I would have local people manage the business. Being global means that you are really rooted locally.

Do business attitudes differ by country?

All businesses need to make a profit. But an important question is, what is this profit for? If you have an answer, then you know why you work. I am doing well and I want the people around me to be happy. If the only shareholder benefits from the profit, then the company will not prosper. The benefits also need to be shared with the staff. That is a business with "big love," so that my staff can lead happier lives.

Do you think this view of Chinese business is understood in the West?

The growth of Chinese businesses and the expansion globally is not just about copying and making fakes. Chinese business is about doing something that provides personal satisfaction. It's like when we eat. We choose something that appeals to our palate, that tastes good, that's good for our body and that makes us happy.

Many Chinese entrepreneurs think this way. They want to become successful, of course, but they have other motives, too. I think that people in the West often don't understand this motivation not only to succeed materially, but also to succeed at something that feels personally rewarding.

" The growth of Chinese businesses and the expansion globally is not just about copying and making fakes. Chinese business is about doing something that provides personal satisfaction. "

SPRING AIRLINES
China-sss.com

行李规定

1. 持P、P1、P2等特价套餐产品的旅客托运行李需收费。您可通过春秋官网china-sss.com购办客和台购买一份重10公斤的托运行李额。

2. 其他旅客的免费行李额 包括托运 李及免托运行李的总重量 并。 起重超分需多件重量小 李额。

3. 所有舱位的旅客可带人身和个 行李 只限带一件 体积不超（70cm × 30cm × 40cm 且总量不超10 。 各免费行李额内。 细则请参看官网说明。

Baggage instruction

1. Spring SuperSaver fares no longer include a free check-in baggage allowance. SuperSaver passengers may purchase a 10kg allowance at SpringAirlines.com or the airport ticketing counter.

2. All other passengers are entitled to a free baggage allowance of 15kg in total (including checked and carry-on baggage). Excess baggage shall be charged at the standard rate per kg.

3. Each passenger is permitted one article of carry-on baggage no larger than 20cmx30cmx40cm and weighing no more than 7kg. For further details please visit SpringAirlines.com

公共柜台/自助行李交运
Self Check-in Bag Drop

41 值机柜台 CHECK-IN

Spring Airlines

旅游

Travel

CHAIRMAN	WANG ZHENGHUA
INDUSTRY	AIRLINES
OWNERSHIP	PRIVATE
SALES (2012)	RMB 11.1 BILLION ($1.8 BILLION)
HEADQUARTERS	SHANGHAI
YEAR FORMED	2004

Spring Airlines is a leading Chinese low-cost carrier. The company's stated mission is to make air travel affordable and available for more people throughout China.

Young people comprise the core customer base, which the airline attempts to reach with innovative online marketing, including a major presence in Chinese social media.

Spring operates 50 routes, mostly connecting domestic cities, but the airline also flies to Japan and Thailand, as well as to Hong Kong and Macau. The company has major operations in Shanghai, Beijing and Shenyang.

A subsidiary of Shanghai International Travel Service, Spring Airlines received government approval in 2004 and began operations in 2005. Shortened to Spring Airlines in English, the name in Chinese characters is Spring and Autumn Airlines.

Spring Airlines area at Shanghai Hongqiao Airport.

CONTEXT INSIGHT
★

Air Travel

Air travel booming both domestically and internationally

Air travel in China is booming, both to domestic and international destinations.

China is expected to become the world's number one tourist destination and number four in outbound travel by 2015, according to the World Tourism Organisation. The country already has the world's second largest domestic airline network, after the United States.

The number of air passengers carried by Chinese domestic and international carriers reached 318.5 million in 2012, up from 191.0 million in 2008, an increase of 66 per cent over five years, according to the World Bank. In contrast, passenger traffic for the United States, the world leader, grew only 5 per cent during the same period, reaching 736.6 million in 2012.

The highest concentration of air travel takes place during two traditional holiday periods, the fall Golden Week and the Chinese New Year, in early winter, when businesses and schools close and people spend time with family or vacationing. At these times the number of people flying almost doubles and most flights are full.

The majority of air passengers, 64.5 per cent are relatively young, age 20 to 40 and predominately male. But over the past five years, the number of people travelling for personal reasons rather than business has increased. And more people from lower tier cities are travelling by air as their incomes rise and airlines expand service.

The rapidly expanding market is drawing competition from United States and European low-cost carriers. The need for government approval and the lack of terminals at major airports has slowed their market entrance so far.

Research and analysis by Millward Brown, a WPP company

CHAIRMAN
WANG ZHENGHUA

State worker becomes leading entrepreneur

Chinese fly high on his dreams

> 66 China has many low-income people who have never flown on an airplane. Perhaps it is their dream to fly, but they can't afford the fare. It's my dream to help them fly. 99

Wang was six years old in 1949, when Mao formed the Peoples Republic of China.

He worked in government until age 40, leaving in the early 1980s, around the time when the reforms of Deng Xiaoping permitted individuals to operate small businesses.

With the opening of China, tourism boomed. The number of foreign visitors surged from 300,000 in 1979 to almost 1.5 million by the mid-1980s. Wang established Shanghai Spring International Travel Service. Today, about 30 million foreign visitors arrive annually in China and Wang is one of China's most successful entrepreneurs.

"Working for the government meant following orders." Wang said. "In business, you can make your own decisions."

He focusses on Chinese travellers whose increased income enables them to fly. By 1994, his agency ranked first in domestic travel in China and he began to plan the next strategic step.

After studying the United States and European travel businesses, Wang concluded that the expanding industry could be divided into three categories:

credit card and banking services, conference companies and charter flight airlines.

The first two categories were state controlled, so Wang decided to launch a charter flight airline. He started modestly, in 1997 and within seven years operated more than 30,000 charter flights, most of them filled to capacity. The government granted him a licence to operate an airline.

Wang again studied western models— Southwest Airlines and Ryan Air among others. He initially marketed Spring Airlines to the younger generation that grew up during China's economic boom and is comfortable with air travel. Sales continue to increase 10-to-20 per cent annually. But Wang has another dream.

At age 70, at a time when others retire, Wang arrives for work early each morning to begin the day on basketball courts in back of the Spring Airlines headquarters, practising tai chi and contemplating the next 10 years of company growth.

"China has many low-income people who have never flown on an airplane. Perhaps it is their dream to fly, but they can't afford the fare. It's my dream to help them fly."

IN HIS OWN WORDS

问答
Q&A

Q&A with Chairman Wang Zhenghua

PERSPECTIVE ON A CHINESE COMPANY

What is the essence of the Spring Airlines brand?

The most important aspect is safety. We invest heavily in our pilots and other professionals who guarantee the safety of the airline. Second is low cost. After that we try to create something special.

Our target customer is young. In fact, about 80 per cent of our ticket sales happen online. And we've created programmes and marketing communications aimed at young people.

How do you staff the cabin crew to best represent the brand?

Salaries are important to attract the best talent. But there's another factor, which is the spirit in the workplace and the opportunities provided. We like to find people with career ambitions and then we try to create conditions that will help them grow with us. We like people who challenge the status quo to obtain their dreams.

How do you reach young people, your target customers and keep them loyal?

First, we try to reach young people in ways that appeal to them. We promote the brand and sell tickets online and we sponsor events, like concerts, to build brand exposure. We have over two million followers on Weibo (the Chinese social media equivalent to Facebook and Twitter).

And we try to understand our young customers and project a youthful attitude. We enable passengers to share personal information when they book a flight. This way, passengers willing to provide personal information can find a good match when they select their seats.

Where do these innovative ideas come from?

We have a professional marketing team. And we have people who specialise in Weibo. They research worldwide to understand the latest trends and to learn what's popular with young people. They present ideas that we discuss and decide whether or not to adopt them.

The red sash worn by the greeter at check-in says, "Welcome."

PEOPLE

Our employees grow with us

"

Of course it's important to guarantee competitive salaries. But beyond that, a company must create a work environment where people feel like they can fulfil their ambitions and advance their careers. I feel that a lot of people want to grow with us and I like to help them grow. I encourage our people to strive for these qualities: to work hard, have vision and be frugal. "

KEEPING PACE WITH RAPID CHANGE

How do you keep your youthful perspective?

I am 70 years old. But my heart and my attitude are much younger. I still have a lot of energy and ambition. I read and keep up with the latest business developments in an effort to understand what will be important in the future.

Because I keep a young mind and heart and I still have many dreams, I can attract and keep a young team. And together we can build something different.

How do you see the future for Spring Airlines?

I look forward to continuing our strong growth. Since our founding in 2004, we have achieved our 10-year plan and we continue to grow at a steady rate, usually 20-to-30 per cent annual increases in sales. That's because we have very clear market positioning.

How will you be able to sustain a rapid growth rate as the company gets larger?

There are two ways to achieve it. One is organically. The other is through acquisition. Some people today are tempted to take steps in directions they're not good at because they think they can make money, at least short term.

This way is not our way. We will continue to focus on what we do well. We will expand within our core business, adding new products and services that we think match our strengths.

Looking back over the past 30 years, what are you most proud of?

I still believe that if you work hard you create value. Don't waste your time or your talent. Everything can be possible but it depends on the individual to make the effort. This is the advice that I give to my staff and they are doing well.

What dreams remain for you?

I had a dream when I began this business and it remains a strong motivator for me. China has many low-income people who have never flown on an airplane. Perhaps it is their dream to fly someday, but they don't have the money. It's my dream to help them fly. I will achieve this dream as I have achieved other dreams—with hard work.

Check-in counter at Shanghai Hongqiao Airport.

NUANCE
INSIGHT

[Industrious]

The character 勤 means industrious and hard working. It is probably the single character used most often to describe the Chinese people. The one character suggests that everything is achievable through hard work.

Industriousness is a core value for many of the business leaders in this report. Chairman Wang says that industriousness is in the DNA of the best Chinese companies and a competitive advantage.

> " We will continue to focus on what we do well. We will expand within our core business, adding new products and services that we think match our strengths. "

CHINA AND THE WEST

What values drive the business?

We encourage people to work hard, that's number one. Second, we want people to have foresight, to plan ahead. Third, we believe in being frugal. We don't like extravagance.

And we want people who are devoted to what they do, who make a contribution to the enterprise. I try to influence people in our company to follow these values.

What brands to you admire?

I like America's Southwest Airline. And I like Ryanair in Europe. These airlines have innovative ideas and effective cost controls. Domestically, I like Xiamen Airline because of its low cost structure and profitability.

> 66
> As societies prosper people have more money and time for other interests, like entertainment. Until then the main focus is work. That's where China is today. That work ethic characterises Chinese companies. 99

How are you adapting your knowledge of western airlines to China?

When I started in the tourism business in the 1980s, I looked to Europe and the United States for the roadmap of that industry. Today's airline industry in Europe and the United States is our future.

The popularity of low cost airlines in Europe and the United States signals the trend of the next 10 years in China. To adapt this model for China I will consider Chinese culture, the needs of our customers and the government regulations.

What can the West learn from Chinese businesses?

Study the best Chinese companies. You will discover that they share the same DNA. They are motivated and work hard. We are still at a relatively early development stage, perhaps similar to where Japan was in the 1950s.

As societies prosper people have more money and time for other interests, like entertainment. Until then the main focus is work. That's where China is today. That work ethic characterises Chinese companies.

Chairman Wang in his office.

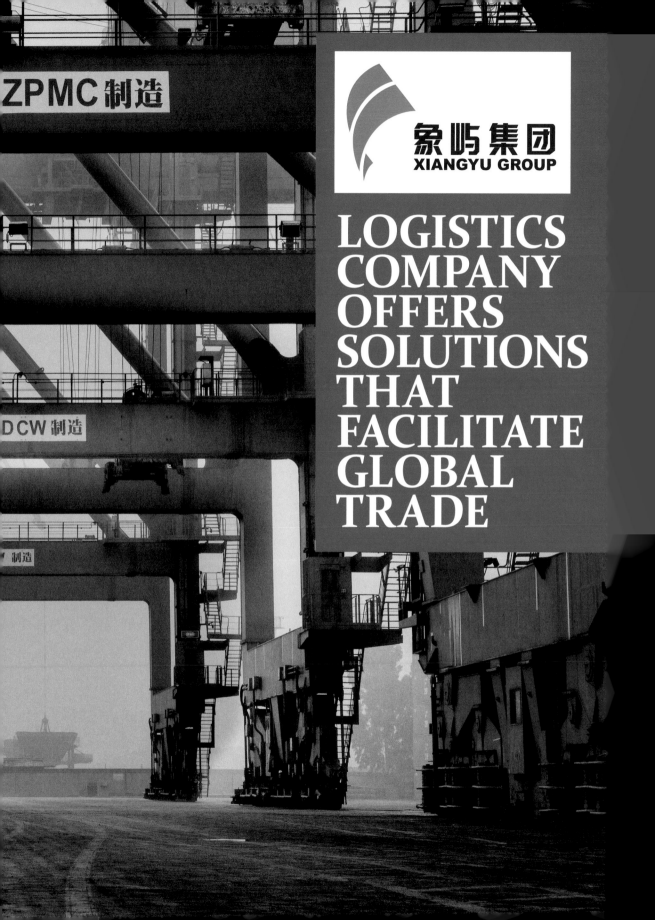

象屿集团
XIANGYU GROUP

LOGISTICS COMPANY OFFERS SOLUTIONS THAT FACILITATE GLOBAL TRADE

Xiamen Xiangyu Group Corporation

贸易
Trading

CHAIRMAN	WANG LONGCHU
INDUSTRY	CONGLOMERATE
OWNERSHIP	LOCAL SOE
SALES (2012)	RMB 40 BILLION ($6.5 BILLION)
HEADQUARTERS	XIAMEN
YEAR FORMED	1995

Xiangyu Group is an SOE conglomerate established by the city Xiamen, in 1995, to develop and operate the Xiamen Xiangyu Free Trade Zone and attract investment to Fujin Province.

The Group primarily integrates logistics support, financing and other offerings into full-service solutions that help customers minimise risk and maximise efficiency at every level along their supply chains.

It operates 85 subsidiaries in these businesses: distribution of commodities, logistics, real estate development and financial services. The company employs roughly 4,000 people.

Following a brief slowdown during the global financial crisis rapid growth has resumed and the company is focussed on increasing margins.

CHAIRMAN
WANG LONGCHU

Supply chain solutions benefit trade customers

Government experience informs company chairman

Wang Longchu joined Xiangyu Group in 1996, soon after its creation by the local government where Wang was an official. Recently promoted to chairman of Xiangyu, he is responsible for 4,000 employees and growth of a business primarily focussed on trade and logistics in the Port of Xiamen.

Maritime traders have been entering this port from many parts of the world since at least the fifteenth century. After a period of closure, the port reopened to the world in 1980, when the administration of Deng Xiaoping established Xiamen as one of the four original Special Economic Zones.

Working for the government at the time, on the effort to open Fujian Province to international trade, Wang gained experience integrating government policy and a market-oriented economy. He still faced challenges when he shifted from his government post to Xiangyu Group, a local SOE.

"We were set up with one purpose— to attract inward investment to Fujin Province and support the businesses of Fujin and take their value to the world," said Wang. "The start was just about survival. We just did our best. We made a lot of mistakes. It was difficult to attract investment. It took us seven years to get any return on our investment in the infrastructure, plant and machinery we set up."

Today, after a slowdown during the global financial crisis, the company continues to grow rapidly. It's introducing a financial services division and upgrading its e-commerce platform as part of a strategy to offer clients full-service support around logistics and supply chain management.

"We take a fully integrated approach so that we can manage all the risks in the business," said Wang. "Everyone should benefit from what we do in a win-win way. We need to consider the whole at all times, not just the thing in front of us."

> 66 The start was just about survival. We just did our best. We made a lot of mistakes. It was difficult to attract investment. 99

IN HIS OWN WORDS

问答
Q&A

Q&A with Chairman Wang Longchu

PERSPECTIVE ON A CHINESE COMPANY

What is the main benefit you provide your customers?

Our core business is logistics and that's not going to change. We simplify logistics for our customers by integrating resources into total solutions. There are risks at every point along the supply chain. Because of experience we can anticipate those risks and help our customers avoid problems.

We need to focus on our social responsibility as well. All stakeholders should benefit from the things we do. It is about a win-win philosophy. In 2011, we initiated our green supply chain services.

Is the business performing well?

The global economic downturn hit us hard. But we have moved on. Last year we did OK. We recently opened a new financial services arm to help the local business community gain access to capital.

We have invested in a new e-commerce platform. Because we offer these services as a package, our customers do not have to worry about the details and they can concentrate on making their businesses efficient.

How is the business changing?

The priorities for our next phase are margin improvement and sustainable, resilient profitability. Government incentives drove our history. That has now changed, so we need to transform our business models to meet this change. We need to consider the domestic demand as our primary focus.

Our key task now is to drive customer value from the state-of-the-art e-commerce and IT systems we have developed and invested in. For perhaps the last 17 years we have focussed on growth for growth's sake. We now need to consolidate, integrate and drive ruthless efficiency from the new investments.

> " Government incentives drove our history. That has now changed, so we need to transform our business models to meet this change. We need to consider the domestic demand as our primary focus. "

KEEPING PACE WITH RAPID CHANGE

Where will growth come from next?

China is big and demand is great, but we are really in the early stages of development. We are just getting started. Government policy is fine. We are here to ensure it gets translated into action on the ground. We are not doing this for the glory of profit. This is about the fundamentals of the economy.

Our growth in some ways has been too fast. Sometimes we didn't know what we were doing right and what we were doing wrong. We just held on to survive the ride. The next five years we will see more organic growth.

How do you manage this constant change?

I simply have some very clear aims and objectives and my approach is to learn from the teams that run the different segments of the business. Then I try to motivate them to achieve their dreams and goals for the business. I do not touch operations at all.

I studied Chinese literature. I understand that people are formed by their upbringing. Everyone deserves respect. To motivate people I try not to issue orders but rather encourage people so they bring passion to a job. We have many staff events where, by observing how people perform and relate, we can form teams.

How do you get the skilled people you need in the business?

The KPIs (Key Performance Indicators) are around their qualifications, but I am also interested in people's hobbies and outside interests. Do they demonstrate that they listen to others and respect their opinions? We need a real mix of people across the business so we need to consider all sorts of different talents. This means respect for others and for their skills and abilities is very important.

CHINA AND THE WEST

What do you consider particular about the Chinese way of doing business?

It is built on Confucian and Buddhist thinking and ways. We think from the inside to the outside, the middle way. We have learned to be very resilient through our hard history. We want to not only win profits, but also do good things for China. I'm in my 50s. People my age were educated to believe that team honour comes before personal achievement. The group is first and the individual is second. This is the Chinese business way.

What is the essential contrast with the West?

It is very important to have balance between the head and the heart. Chinese business is about balance, much more so than I see in the West. We have a long history and 5,000 years of culture to build on. This gives us an intangible competitive advantage and a positive and generally balanced perspective on the things we do and our thinking about the future.

How will these Chinese attitudes impact the future?

China will have a greater effect on the world in the years to come, both economic and cultural. Our influence on the global economy is becoming greater and greater. In the world of the Top 100 luxury brands there is not one that is Chinese. If we can get some Chinese brands to a high level of maturity then we will have a very positive future. There will be changes in China, too. After this 30-year period of rapid growth, we're looking to reclaim our ancient culture.

How ready do you think the world is for this change in China?

The world is not ready at all. The world doesn't understand China. The West thinks it does, but it doesn't. Western people do not understand the Chinese ways. The world does not come to China to learn our ways.

On break in the Xiangyu staff room at Xiamen Port (above) and Xiangyu workers in transportation shed at Xiamen Port.

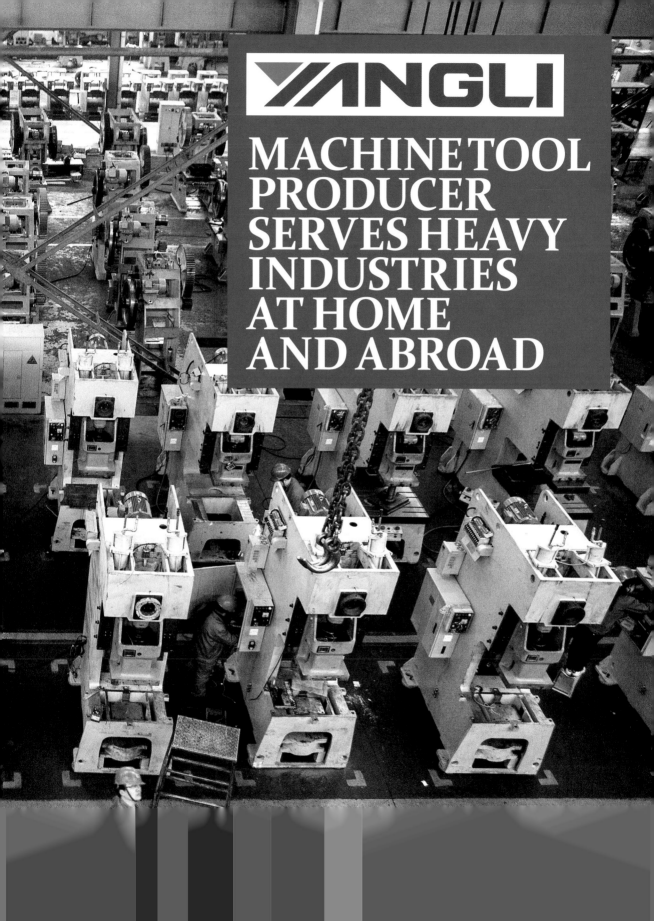

YANGLI

MACHINE TOOL PRODUCER SERVES HEAVY INDUSTRIES AT HOME AND ABROAD

Jiangsu Yangli Group Company, Ltd.

制造业
Manufacturing

CHAIRMAN	LIN GUOFU
INDUSTRY	MACHINE TOOL MANUFACTURING
OWNERSHIP	JOINT-STOCK COMPANY
SALES (2012)	RMB 2.51 BILLION ($410 MILLION)
HEADQUARTERS	YANGZHOU
YEAR FORMED	1966

Yangli designs and manufactures metal casting equipment, precision die presses and other machine tools for heavy industries, including automotive, aerospace and electronic appliances.

The company was established as a local enterprise of Yangzhou, a city in the Yangtze Delta, where Yangli opened its first plant in 1966. Economic difficulty characterised its formative years and the company was insolvent by the early 1980s, when the government of Deng Xiaoping introduced economic reforms.

After the opening of China, Yangli recovered rapidly, restructuring to become a joint-stock company and the largest business in Yangzhou's Hanjiang Economic Development Zone. The company has expanded through acquisition and the formation of five subsidiaries.

It also established research and development centres to explore innovations in machinery including heavy-duty presses, precision presses and hydraulic equipment. The company maintains relationships with similar research institutes in other regions of the world.

Today, it operates five plants and sells its products throughout China and worldwide, with a substantial presence in Europe, North America and Southeast Asia. The company employs 5,000 people. It maintains around 100 branch offices. Overseas sales total approximately 15 per cent of revenue.

Monitoring equipment.

CONTEXT INSIGHT

★

Manufacturing

Tool manufacturing drives economic growth, but faces competition

The machine tool manufacturing industry is an important engine of China's economy. It has achieved 10 consecutive years of rapid growth since 2002, making China the world's largest machine tool producer in output value, in 2009.

Still, certain structural problems persist. Most Chinese machine tool manufacturers are engaged at the low end of the market, creating overcapacity. Taiwanese and South Korean companies occupy the mid-market, with the high end mostly served by makers from Japan, Germany and the United States.

Committed to the use of state-of-the art technologies, the Yangli Group has set the pace for China's forging machine tool industry and enhanced its competitive standing both at home and abroad. It's been an industry leader in sales and profit.

A project known as "116," launched in 2009, has been a key to Yangli's recent success. The number signifies that the project was a first priority and involved upgrading 16 traditional projects with high market value.

In addition, Yangli has established a technologically advanced research centre, including research and development concentrations for five of its major product categories. It also maintains alliances with important academic research institutes.

Source: Millward Brown, a WPP company

CHAIRMAN
LIN GUOFU

Youngest apprentice advances to chairman

47-year career parallels the history of modern China

Lin Guofu began working at Yangli in September 1966, when the first plant opened and the same month that Mao's government shut schools throughout China, encouraging students to join the Red Guard of the Cultural Revolution to strengthen the political orthodoxy.

Just 16, Lin was the company's youngest apprentice. By age 30, he was head of production and he became plant director before turning 35. Now he's chairman and CEO, with a 47-year career at a company that he helped build and whose history parallels the remarkable development of modern China.

Lin views his career in stages. His foundational years of learning the business depended on the far-sighted company director, an intellectual who attached great importance to education and established formal training for young employees.

"He sent us for a paid training course for three-to-six months in Shanghai and Wuxi, which was rarely seen in those years," Lin recalled.

By the early 1980s, with China suffering economically, the business almost failed. It recovered during the period of reform and opening led by Deng Xiaoping and by the end of the 1990s Yangli was a successful machine tool company with over 1,000 employees, the largest local enterprise of its kind, with a growing global presence.

Lin influenced the development of Yangli, shaping a culture that values employees and emphasises continuous improvement. "I am 63 years old," he said. "I'd like to work another 13 years and help Yangli grow more competitive, with constant innovation and high-end products."

He draws inspiration from Kong Ming, a clever Chinese military strategist who, according to one story, outmanoeuvred a much better equipped army, almost 2,000 years ago, by tricking its archers to fire all their arrows into decoy soldiers made of straw.

"After I'm 76, I'd like to travel around the world to gain a deeper understanding of western cultures," said Lin, "staying in the United Kingdom and Ireland for a while and reading more world history."

" I am 63 years old. I'd like to work another 13 years and help Yangli grow more competitive, with constant innovation and high-end products. "

IN HIS OWN WORDS

问答

Q&A

Q&A with Chairman Lin Guofu

PERSPECTIVE ON A CHINESE COMPANY

What is your first priority in running the business?

Our employees come first. We think of our people as our most important asset, much more important than plant or equipment, which is the basis of a manufacturing company like ours. We consider ourselves an employee-focussed business and we see our employees as friends.

This view is part of a larger hierarchy that drives the integrity of the business. The welfare of the employees is first. Next are the positive relationships we maintain with our customers and our good faith efforts to meet their needs. Finally, we feel a deep responsibility to the welfare of the society.

What values or principles drive the company?

We must dare to face our own weaknesses and keep correcting them. Sustained competitiveness depends on strengthening ourselves. First, we must be self-aware and willing to identify our weaknesses. Second, we must have the courage and motivation to improve.

These principles apply to both ourselves as individuals and business people and also to the enterprises that we manage. We need to continually improve our core competencies, including company strategy, management philosophy and operations.

How do you anticipate or cope with change?

Our growth requires that we always look ahead to be aware of change and adapt as necessary. This attitude is particularly important in two areas: management and technology. We need to keep pace with the latest management approaches so that we are always operating the business at an optimal level. And we need to constantly invest in the latest technology because producing excellent industrial machinery is our core business.

JIANGSU YANGLI GROUP COMPANY, LTD.

Worker with machine presses.

NUANCE
INSIGHT

鐵飯碗
[A stable job]

When asked about his first priority in running Yangli, Chairman Lin said that people, employees, are most important. While his answer may sound like a familiar western response, it contains a meaning deeply rooted in the Chinese psyche. Two of the characters that comprise the word for a stable job, 饭碗, can also mean food bowl, which is a metaphor for livelihood. During China's long history, when the majority of people endured crushing poverty, a job guaranteed the next meal or life itself. A stable job is often referred to as 铁饭碗, meaning an iron bowl, an indestructible vessel.

KEEPING PACE WITH RAPID CHANGE

How is China's business environment changing?

China's rapid economic development during the past 30 years depended in part on government policy favouring growth. Businesses benefited from low-cost labour, materials and production as well as tax incentives. Those days are over. Government priorities have changed.

Today, there is much more discussion about letting people enjoy the dividend of those 30 years of reform and opening-up. The question is, where is this dividend? It doesn't come from local or central government. Rather, it comes from businesses operating more efficiently and increasing value.

How does this ongoing change in the business environment challenge Yangli?

Two idioms summarise how we've responded to change in the past. One is, "Keep pace with the times," and the other is, "Creep before you walk." The former phrase advises us to continue accumulating knowledge and experience. The latter phrase points to a style for gaining that knowledge and experience in step-by-step increments.

Deep understanding of the two phrases played an important role in building a solid foundation for the company and in developing the corporate culture, strategy and management principles. Sustained success requires balance and measured progress. We will continue this approach.

What's the role of innovation?

I am eager to have Yangli grow stronger and more competitive. This improvement will require innovation in both manufacturing and operations. The key questions are: How can Yangli become a high-end products manufacturer; and how can we improve product performance more quickly?

For example and without becoming too technical, we can optimise some of our machinery to improve performance and energy-efficiency and we are taking these steps. We act responsibly about industrial emissions. In manufacturing processes we employ cutting-edge technology to protect the environment.

*Surveying the factory floor (above)
and checking machinery.*

> " China's rapid
> economic development during
> the past 30 years depended in
> part on government policy favouring
> growth. Businesses benefitted
> from low-cost labour,
> materials and production
> as well as tax incentives.
> Those days are over. "

CHINA AND THE WEST

How do you view the state of understanding between China and the West?

Mutual understanding is important for guiding future business interaction and success, but it is lacking. To Chinese people, the United States and Europe seem ambivalent toward China. They want to engage, but they also have concerns.

Both China and the West need to be more open minded about trying to understand each other more deeply. This relationship between China and the West is an important topic for research and study.

How would you explain China to the West?

China has become the world's second-largest economy and will catch up with the United States in the next 10 years. For both the United States and Europe this raises the question of how best to respond.

Western countries might be less concerned about this question if they had more knowledge of the history of China. They don't comprehend the full meaning behind the "great rejuvenation of China."

What does the term "great rejuvenation" mean to you?

The phrase "rise of China" could mean that China's development is simply a recent phenomenon. The word "rejuvenation," however, connotes our long history and prior periods when the country enjoyed great stature. For example, about 1,000 years ago, Yangzhou was a prosperous urban centre, the New York, London or Paris of its day.

How does history affect today's China?

China was an advanced civilisation even more than 2000 years ago. With the creation of the Silk Road, the overland and maritime routes connecting East and West, the Chinese exchanged art and technologies with other peoples. In more modern times China has suffered hardship and setbacks. This long and profound history is the strong foundation of China's rapid rejuvenation, which now is being realised through hard work.

" Mutual understanding is important for guiding future business interaction and success, but it is lacking. To Chinese people, the United States and Europe seem ambivalent toward China. They want to engage, but they also have concerns. "

Inspecting an electrical switch.

WORLDWIDE PROMOTION RAISES BRAND PROFILE OF BEIJING BEER

Beijing Yanjing Brewery Company, Ltd.

CHAIRMAN	LI FUCHENG
INDUSTRY	BEER
OWNERSHIP	LOCAL SOE
SALES (2013)	RMB 13.0 BILLION ($2.1 BILLION)
HEADQUARTERS	BEIJING
YEAR FORMED	1980

Yanjing is one of China's largest beer brands, named for the ancient capital that occupied the area now called Beijing.

The first Yanjing brewery opened in Beijing, during 1980, as the government of Deng Xiaoping launched its market reforms. Yanjing produced 10,000 tonnes of beer that year. Today it produces 5.5 million tonnes annually from 40 facilities in 18 provinces throughout China.

The brand captures about an 85 per cent share of the Beijing beer market. It's also strong in Guangxi and Hunan provinces and Inner Mongolia. The Yanjing brand is positioned as "green food" with environmentally responsible brewing practices, including the quality and safety of the water used.

Yanjing was an official sponsor of the 2008 Beijing Olympics and sponsored Beijing Culture Week in London during the 2012 Summer Games. The brand is ranked number 40 in the BrandZ™ Top 50 Most Valuable Chinese Brands 2013.

Beijing Yanjing Brewery Company Ltd. was listed on the Shenzhen Stock Exchange in 1997. It is part of Beijing Enterprises Holdings Ltd., whose other interests include energy and water treatment. The company employs 40,000 people.

Delivering Yanjing to a Beijing restaurant.

INSIGHT

Beer Industry

Growth potential strong in the world's largest beer market

China is the world's largest beer market, roughly twice the size of the second largest market, the United States. The vast size of the nation's population, along with relatively low per-person consumption, signals a significant growth opportunity.

The opportunity has attracted foreign competition and stimulated a lot of merger, acquisition and joint venture activity. As a result, the distinction between multinational, national and local status can be unclear. The top five category leaders, for example, include both independent Chinese and foreign-backed brands.

Foreign brands remain concentrated in the small but rapidly growing premium segment. Local brands dominate overall. The top three brands—Snow, Tsingtao and Yanjing—accounted for almost one-third of national sales in 2012. All three brands experienced exceptional growth in recent years.

Yanjing remains the only Chinese brand without the backing of a foreign brewer. Global brewer SABMiller plc has a stake in Snow and Japan's Asahi Breweries Ltd. has invested in Tsingtao. This does not mean that Yanjing lacks global aspirations. Yanjing aims to become a leading international player and is investing heavily in greater output and marketing initiatives.

Over the past few years, Yanjing acquired multiple domestic breweries and boosted the capacity of existing facilities. Marketing efforts include sponsorship of sports and scientific activities, such as the Chinese Table Tennis Association and the China Lunar Exploration Programme. Yanjing exports to many international markets.

CONSUMERS CONSIDER AND TRY YANJING

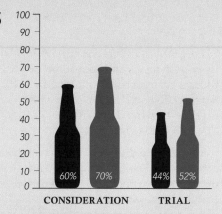

▮ 2008   ▮ 2013

CONSIDERATION — 60% 70%
TRIAL — 44% 52%

The number of Chinese consumers saying they would consider purchasing Yanjing increased 10 percentage points between 2008 and 2013, while the number of people who said they had tried the brand increased 8 percentage points over the same period.

Research and analysis by Millward Brown, a WPP company

CHAIRMAN
LI FUCHENG

> 66 I am always thinking, what is the brand? What are the attributes of a brand? The strength of a brand is equal to its quality and the strength of brand equates to the strength of its reputation. 99

Beijing native builds local beer brand

Contributes to growth of company and country

Born and raised in Beijing, Li Fucheng remembers the day, in September 1980, when his employer, Yanjing beer, broke ground in Beijing for its first brewery. Today, Li is chairman of the company.

His personal history, the growth of the Yanjing brand and the development of the Chinese beer industry are intertwined. In 2008, to mark the thirtieth anniversary of China's opening up, China Central Television (CCTV) included Li among 30 individuals honoured for their contributions to China's economic growth.

Three years later CCTV again recognised Li for his leadership in building Chinese brands. In his open and energetic style Li personifies the qualities of the popular Yanjing brand. He is not only chairman, but also the brand's best ambassador.

"I am always thinking, what is the brand? What are the attributes of a brand? The strength of a brand is equal to its quality and the strength of brand equates to the strength of its reputation."

Proud that the Yanjing brand has grown without the joint venture partnerships that propelled many other Chinese beer brands, Li doesn't rule out a corporate marriage in the future, but stresses Yanjing's self-reliance.

The brand enjoys access to capital and to the latest technology, two necessities that Chinese brands often seek from foreign partners. A third factor, access to overseas markets, is not an immediate concern for Li. He first wants to first build the Yanjing brand across China.

"If there is no brand, then a company doesn't have a competitive advantage," said Li. "A company without a brand is a company in a precarious position."

IN HIS OWN WORDS

问答
Q&A

Q&A with Chairman Li Fucheng

PERSPECTIVE ON A CHINESE COMPANY

What is the essence of the Yanjing brand?

The essence is in the name. Yanjing is an ancient capital city and an early name of the place now known as Beijing. The Chinese character for the swallow is part of the Yanjing name. Our logo features an abstract image of this bird, a symbol of hope and renewal. It emphasises the connection of the brand with the place.

We created Yanjing as a local brand in the Shunyi district on the outskirts of Beijing. We first became a famous brand in the city and then throughout China. We aspire to be a strong international brand and I believe we can accomplish this goal. Most of the major global brands were first leaders in their domestic markets.

How do you build the brand to achieve this goal?

Sponsorships are an important part of our strategy. Yanjing was an official sponsor of the 2008 Beijing Olympics. At the London Summer Games, in 2012, we held a week long promotional event. Our international aspirations are communicated on our label in a short poem that I personally wrote. It says in part, "Springtime swallows spread their wings and soar over the seven seas."

In what other ways do you communicate global ambition?

We have a two-part slogan: "Inspire the world. Exceed the dream." Each part of the slogan has three meanings. The word "inspire" refers to the last 30 years of China's development, which is a positive example for the world. It also refers to the fact that China changed from a weak competitor in international sports to a nation that produces champions.

The final reference is about Yanjing and how our rapid growth draws the respect of the industry. Contained in the word "exceed" are three references to how we want to surpass our rate of growth, continue to innovate and endure to become a century-old company someday.

> " We aspire to be a strong international brand and I believe we can accomplish this goal. Most of the major global brands were first leaders in their domestic markets. "

Yanjing drinkers in Beijing.

BRAND POWER

Loyal customer solves visa hitch

Several years ago, Yanjing Chairman Li Fucheng, along with several other company executives and Chinese government officials, travelled together overseas to close a major international trade arrangement in Finland.

Because of a misunderstanding they were detained in Budapest, their last stop before a short flight to Finland and the official contract signing. Immigration requested new visas, but it was late on a Friday afternoon.

"We hurried to the Finnish embassy and I gave my business card to the visa officer," Li recalled. "The officer asked, 'You're the big boss of Yanjing? Yanjing was my favourite beer when I was stationed at the Finnish embassy in Beijing.'"

The official approved visas for Li and the other Yanjing executives but not for the Chinese government officials. Li explained that it would be a serious breach of protocol to attend the contract signing without them.

The visa official consulted with his supervisor and, with just minutes to spare, the entire group boarded a flight to Finland. "The episode," said Li, "is an inspiring lesson about the power of brand."

KEEPING PACE WITH RAPID CHANGE

How do you differentiate in such a competitive business?

Brand and corporate values are key. We believe that we must face our employees and our customers with a human heart. It's important to be an honest and good person. And we must always have integrity when doing business.

We communicate these values to our employees. We stress that product quality is important and it's everyone's responsibility. I can reduce all the aspects of running the business to one truth or principle. It is possible to win short-term advantage by being cleverer than the competition, but sustained success depends on consistent ethical behaviour.

What is the number one requirement for success?

Talent is the core. Without talent, it is hard to gain a competitive advantage. But it's critical to manage talent effectively. There are several dimensions. First, the organisational structure must be well designed so that people are clear about their responsibilities. Performance measures should cover key areas, including both planning and execution.

What characteristics do you look for in employees?

Both general intelligence (IQ) and emotional intelligence (EQ) are important. High IQ people may be systematic and organised and also have strong analytical ability. But sometimes people with high

IQ focus too narrowly on small details. No one in business wants to deal with that kind of personality. I don't have a high IQ but my EQ is good. It helps me work smoothly with others, particularly those with similar EQ. And together we deal with business problems.

We like to employ people who fully dedicate themselves to the company, meaning that they put the interests of the company ahead of their own. They should appreciate, with all their heart, the pioneering spirit of Yanjing and our history and traditions.

Can you describe an ideal employee?

The most desirable employees are not afraid of facing challenges. They're self confident and willing to take reasonable risks. At the same time, they carry out their duties with modesty and frugality. These employees are able to win the customer's heart and sustain our strong brand.

How do you motivate people?

It's important to have thoughtful and well-communicated KPIs (Key Performance Indicators) and to provide appropriate incentives for achieving goals. We link staff compensation to company profit. In fact, the compensation package of our regional directors is four-to-five times greater than mine. We base their compensation on five indicators: revenue and ROI, cash flow and collections, market share, brand improvement and debt levels.

Yanjing served in several Beijing settings.

CHINA AND THE WEST

Where is your immediate growth opportunity?

The domestic Chinese market is enormous and we believe that beer consumption in China will continue to grow. The gap between consumption in China and other markets is large. In the United States, beer drinkers consume 100 litres of beer per year. In the Germany, the level of consumption is 115 litres; in the Czech Republic it's 160 litres. In China, beer drinkers consume only 35 litres per year. As the lives of Chinese people continue to improve, their purchasing power and their beer consumption will rise.

How will you achieve your ambitious growth objectives?

We are now the eighth largest beer company in the world in total production. We want to be ranked number six by 2015. That means increasing our output from 5.5 million tonnes today to 8 million. Half of this additional output will come from a combination of merger and acquisition and construction of new production facilities. We will achieve the other 50 per cent of growth from expanding the capacity of our existing facilities.

What is your attitude regarding the formation of international partnerships?

There are three basics reasons for us to consider a partnership. None of them are relevant today. The first reason is access to capital. We have three listed companies and an excellent credit rating, so capital is not a problem. Second, a partner could supply important technology. We have developed our own world-class technology and production equipment.

Third, a foreign partner could provide rapid access to new markets. We are focussed domestically for the near-term. About 20 years ago, eight of our Beijing-based competitors formed joint ventures. We resisted and we succeeded.

CONTACTS
& CREDITS

CONTACTS

GRANT THORNTON INTERNATIONAL

Grant Thornton is one of the world's leading organisations of independent assurance, tax and advisory firms. These firms help dynamic organisations unlock their potential for growth by providing meaningful, actionable advice through a broad range of services. Proactive teams, led by approachable partners in these firms, use insights, experience and instinct to solve complex issues for privately owned, publicly listed and public sector clients. Over 35,000 Grant Thornton people, in over 100 countries, are focussed on making a difference to clients, colleagues and the communities in which we live and work.

Jonathan Geldart
Global Head - Marketing Communications
Jonathan.Geldart@gti.gt.com
www.grantthornton.com

GRANT THORNTON ZHI TONG

Grant Thornton Zhi Tong has pioneered a unique, integrated organisation for the Chinese market. The "one China, one firm" approach, works seamlessly across China and Hong Kong, forming a network of 17 offices with access to 120 partners and over 2,700 professionals. The company serves a broad base of clients including about 140 public companies, more than 2,000 stated-owned enterprises (SOEs), private companies and multinational companies (MNCs). With the combination of award-winning technical expertise and the intuition, insight and confidence gained from extensive sector experience, Grant Thornton Zhi Tong helps clients unlock their potential for growth.

Kelly Jiang
Chief Marketing Officer
kelly.jiang@cn.gt.com
www.grantthornton.cn

WPP

WPP is the world's largest communications services group with billings of $70.5 billion and revenues of $16.5 billion. Through its operating companies, the Group provides a comprehensive range of advertising and marketing services including advertising and media investment management; data investment management; public relations and public affairs; branding and identity; retail and shopper marketing; healthcare communications; direct, digital, promotion and relationship marketing; and specialist communications. The company employs over 170,000 people (including associates) in over 3,000 offices across 110 countries.

David Roth
CEO The Store WPP, EMEA and Asia
droth@wpp.com
www.wpp.com

MILLWARD BROWN

Millward Brown is one of the world's leading research agencies and is expert in effective advertising, marketing communications, media and brand equity research. Through the use of an integrated suite of validated research solutions — both qualitative and quantitative — Millward Brown helps clients build strong brands and services. Millward Brown has more than 87 offices in 58 countries. Additional practices include Millward Brown's Global Media Practice (media effectiveness unit), Millward Brown Optimor (focussed on helping clients maximise the returns on their brand and marketing investments) and Dynamic Logic (the world leader in digital marketing effectiveness). Millward Brown is part of Kantar, WPP's data investment management and consultancy group.

Doreen Wang Head of Client Solutions
Millward Brown China
doreen.wang@millwardbrown.com
Deepender Rana CEO Greater China
Millward Brown China
deepender.rana@millwardbrown.com
www.millwardbrown.com

WPP IN CHINA

WPP in China employs over 14,000 people in Beijing, Shanghai, Guangzhou and many other cities and provinces. Areas of expertise include: advertising, branding and identity, digital, insight and consultancy, public relations, promotion, marketing, media, retail and shopper marketing. WPP in China provides the knowledge and implementation necessary to understand China and build and sustain brand value.

Bessie Lee
CEO WPP China
blee@wpp.com
www.wpp.com

BRANDZ™

Established in 1998 by WPP and constantly updated, the BrandZ™ database of brand analytics and equity is the world's largest and most authoritative containing over two million consumers interviews about more than 10,000 different brands in over 30 countries. BrandZ™ is proprietary to WPP companies. For further information about BrandZ™ contact any WPP company or:

Graham Staplehurst
Global BrandZ™ Director
graham.staplehurst@millwardbrown.com
www.brandz.com

THE AUTHORS

JONATHAN GELDART

Global Head - Marketing and Communications Grant Thornton International Ltd.

Jonathan.Geldart@gti.gt.com
www.gti.org

Jonathan is responsible for the Grant Thornton global brand. He rebranded the organisation in 2008 and in 2012 launched the globally adopted strapline and brand promise for Grant Thornton – "An Instinct for Growth".

He advises the Grant Thornton organisation around the world on strategy, brand and business development matters. In this regard, he has worked in China for many years as well as in other emerging economies. He rebranded and renamed the Chinese firm Grant Thornton Zhi Tong, in 2012.

Jonathan is a regular speaker on brands, branding and leadership around the world. In 2011, he became the first non-Chinese lecturer on brands and branding at training sessions sponsored by the Chinese government. He is an accredited speaker, writer, teacher and advisor for the CICPA (the Chinese accounting institute) on brand development in the Chinese accounting profession.

A keen outdoor enthusiast, Jonathan trekked to the North Pole in April 2006, has climbed in the Himalayas and is a qualified "mountain leader" and "mountain medic" with the British Mountaineering Council. He is a member of the UK Marketing Society, a Fellow of the UK Institute of Directors, the UK Chartered Institute of Marketing and a Freeman of the Worshipful Company of Marketors in The City of London.

DAVID ROTH

CEO
The Store - WPP
Europe, Middle East, Africa and Asia

droth@wpp.com
www.wpp.com
Blog: www.davidroth.com
Twitter: @davidrothlondon

David is an acknowledged China expert and has been travelling to China for almost two decades and continues to advise retailers, manufacturers and brand owners in many sectors about China, market entry strategies and the changing Chinese consumer.

He started his career at the House of Commons where he worked for a Member of Parliament. Swapping the cut and thrust of politics for the cut and thrust of advertising, David joined Bates Dorland, becoming a main board director for strategy and the managing director of the consulting and digital divisions.

After establishing his own strategy consultancy and working with leading technology and retail brands, David joined Kingfisher's B&Q plc, one of Europe's largest retailers, sitting on the main board of directors as UK and international marketing director. He was a leading member of the project team that developed, launched and ran B&Q home improvement stores in Taiwan, China and Korea.

David joined WPP as CEO of The Store – WPP for EMEA and Asia, WPP's Global Retail Practice. David also leads WPP BrandZ™, the world's largest brand equity study. David is the author of a number of publications including the "Retailing in a Recession" playbook series and "The History of Retail in 100 Objects".

A frequent speaker at international events and lecturer on management development programmes for senior Chinese business leaders and entrepreneurs, David is a non-executive director of TFT, an NGO dedicated to sustainable production and sits on the board of the Centre for International Business and Management of the Judge Business School at the University of Cambridge.

CREDITS

EDITORIAL, PHOTOGRAPHY, AND PRODUCTION

KEN SCHEPT is a professional writer and editor specialising in reports and books about brands and marketing. He helped develop WPP's extensive library of global publications, with special focus on China and Latin America. Prior to launching his freelance career, he covered the retail sector internationally as an editor with a leading US business media publisher.

DANIELA HORNSKOV SUN serves as communications assistant for The Store WPP and manages special projects such as *The Thoughts of Chairmen Now*. Born in China and educated in both China and Europe, she brings language and translation skills along with cultural insights to WPP publishing projects and events.

KELLY JIANG has over 17 years of professional marketing experience. She joined Grand Thornton Zhi Tong in 2011 as chief marketing officer. Her responsibilities include research, branding, marketing, communication and business development. Prior to joining Grand Thornton Zhi Tong, she worked at one of the "Big Four" consultancies for 10 years as director of clients and markets.

PAUL GORDON is a marketing consultant with a background in brand, communications and digital marketing. He has a particular interest in corporate and professional services and is an advisor to Grant Thornton International on a range of strategic marketing activities. China and other emerging markets are Paul's specialities.

CAROLYN CUMMINGS-OSMOND is a senior lecturer in the School of Media at Southampton Solent University. Prior to this position, she was managing editor and new product development manager at educational publishers, Philip and Tacey. As a freelance editor and copywriter, Carolyn has written copy for IBM, The Royal Mint, New Look and other corporate clients.

CECILIE ØSTERGREN is a professional photographer, based in Shanghai, who has worked closely with WPP agencies since 2009. Her documentary and portraiture work includes a project with Added Value on Chinese consumers exhibited at the Houses of Parliament in London. Cecilie's images have appeared in WPP's BrandZ™ reports about brands in China and Latin America. Working with Danish publisher Politikens Forlag she's photographed travel books about India, Greece and Denmark, her native country.

KAY BLEWETT has extensive experience in the design industry, working with a broad spectrum of clients across many sectors, from charities and educational establishments to pharmaceutical companies and government departments. She has spent the last 15 years working principally with some of the UK's leading retailers, as well as with WPP and its operating companies.

ACKNOWLEDGEMENTS

Special thanks and appreciation to Chairman Xu Hua, the leaders, partners and staff of Grant Thornton Zhi Tong without whose support and personal commitment this book would never have had the richness and diversity it does.

A special thanks also to Adrian Gonzalez, Deepender Rana, Doreen Wang, Chirantan Ray, Benoit Garbe, Tiger Shang, Norman Yao and Jonah Brown from Millward Brown China for their insight and support.

We also express our appreciation to Ken Koo for his initial design concepts and to Steve Bale, of the Ogilvy Group, for interviewing and photographing Chairman Li Fucheng of Yanjing Brewery Company, Ltd.